HOME IS WHERE THE HEART IS

MICHAELA TRUEMAN

Silver Devils Publishing

Copyright © 2022 by Michaela Trueman
Cover design by Michaela Trueman & George M Howard

All rights reserved. No part of this book may be reproduced in any manner whatsoever without written permission except in the case of brief quotations embodied in critical articles and reviews.

This is a work of fiction. Unless otherwise indicated, all the names, characters, businesses, places, events and incidents in this book are either the product of the author's imagination or used in a fictitious manner. Any resemblance to actual persons, living or dead, or actual events is purely coincidental or fictitious.

First published: 2022
This edition published: 2023

HOME IS WHERE THE HEART IS

Contents

Dedication   viii

1	Chapter One	1
2	Chapter Two	4
3	Chapter Three	6
4	Chapter Four	10
5	Chapter Five	15
6	Chapter Six	22
7	Chapter Seven	27
8	Chapter Eight	33
9	Chapter Nine	37
10	Chapter Ten	40
11	Chapter Eleven	47
12	Chapter Twelve	52
13	Chapter Thirteen	57
14	Chapter Fourteen	62
15	Chapter Fifteen	65

16	Chapter Sixteen	69
17	Chapter Seventeen	73
18	Chapter Eighteen	78
19	Chapter Nineteen	80
20	Chapter Twenty	88
21	Chapter Twenty-one	93
22	Chapter Twenty-two	97
23	Chapter Twenty-three	104
24	Chapter Twenty-four	109
25	Chapter Twenty-five	114
26	Chapter Twenty-six	119
27	Chapter Twenty-seven	125
28	Chapter Twenty-eight	131
29	Chapter Twenty-nine	140
30	Chapter Thirty	142
31	Chapter Thirty-one	145
32	Chapter Thirty-two	152
33	Chapter Thirty-three	160
34	Chapter Thirty-four	163
35	Chapter Thirty-five	166
36	Chapter Thirty-six	171
37	Chapter Thirty-seven	176
38	Chapter Thirty-eight	182

39	Chapter Thirty-nine	184
40	Chapter Forty	189
41	Chapter Forty-one	192
42	Chapter Forty-two	196
43	Chapter Forty-three	199
44	Chapter Forty-four	202
45	Chapter Forty-five	206
46	Chapter Forty-six	210
47	Chapter Forty-seven	214
48	Chapter Forty-eight	220
49	Chapter Forty-nine	230
50	Chapter Fifty	239

Acknowledgements	245
Other Books By Michaela Trueman	249
Social Media	253
Excerpt	255

For Kerri, a creative and independent woman, not a sea lion.

I

Chapter One

A cosy cottage framed by purple flowers was what Mackenzie found at the address her grandad had given her over the phone. It looked comfortable enough for a man and his granddaughter to live in, and not in need of any work. Pleased that her new home was more than serviceable, Mackenzie approached it.

The combination of her fatigue and the cottage's flowers made it difficult for Mackenzie to locate the key safe her grandad had told her about. When she eventually found the key safe and opened it, Mackenzie was dismayed to find it empty.

The door Mackenzie wanted to get through suddenly opened. For a second or two, she wondered if she'd got the wrong house. Her grandad had said he would be out, and he lived alone. The number by the door matched the one she'd been given over the phone, which suggested it was the right place, and it occurred to her that the key safe was exactly where she'd been told it was.

A woman who looked to be around Mackenzie's age emerged from the cottage and looked her up and down. The woman's gaze lingered on her well-worn leather ankle boots. 'Are *you* Madison?' the woman asked.

'Mackenzie, actually,' Mackenzie replied with her hands on her hips.

'Yes, *that's* what he said! I remember now. Sorry for getting your name wrong. Trust me, I know how annoying that is,' the woman said.

When Mackenzie gave her a blank stare, the woman announced: 'I'm Emma-Leigh. That's *Emma-Leigh*, not *Emily*. I'm your grandad's cleaner.'

Upon finding out that the unexpected occupant of her grandad's house was a cleaner, Mackenzie breathed a sigh of relief. Ever since she'd found the key safe empty, she'd worried someone had stolen the key.

'Hi, *Emma-Leigh*. I won't introduce myself, for it sounds like Grandad already has,' Mackenzie replied, wondering just how much her grandad had told Emma-Leigh.

Emma-Leigh chortled. 'Yes, he did. You're Mackenzie Wight, graduate of Sheffield University and one very bright woman, so I'm told,' she revealed.

As there was nothing she needed to tell Emma-Leigh or ask her, Mackenzie didn't respond.

'Your room is the one to the right of the stairs. I cleaned it this morning and left the window open. It should be clean and fresh for you,' Emma-Leigh told Mackenzie.

'Thanks,' Mackenzie replied.

With a suitcase almost as big as her behind her, Mackenzie entered the house she was to call home. The first thing she noticed were the steep and narrow carpeted stairs. She paused for a moment to prepare herself for the task of hauling the case up the stairs.

'I carry Henry up there. Do you want me to take your suitcase?' Emma-Leigh offered.

'I don't need help. I can do this myself,' Mackenzie replied.

Emma-Leigh frowned. 'If you don't want my help, that's no skin off my nose. I'll be done in ten minutes or so. I'm not supposed to still be here, but I'm a bit behind today,' she said.

As she was focusing on how challenging the stairs were, Mackenzie didn't really hear Emma-Leigh. She just started dragging her case up them, step by step.

By the time Mackenzie reached her bedroom, she was out of breath. That didn't make her regret rejecting Emma-Leigh's offer though.

It wasn't just carrying the suitcase that had exhausted Mackenzie. Spending hours on trains away from her hometown, surrounded by strangers having loud phone calls, coughing, and eating smelly food, had also taken its toll. This made the solid divan double bed in the corner of the room look very inviting. She couldn't resist the temptation to flop down onto it. As her grandad wasn't yet home, and she was too tired to explore the town she'd just moved to, there was nothing to stop her having a nap.

As she laid on the bed, Mackenzie took in her surroundings. Each item of furniture had its own character and story, and no relation to anything else in the room. Nothing had any meaning to her, or any memories associated with it. It was just as Mackenzie had intended.

2

Chapter Two

After greeting her and making tea while ignoring her protests that *she* was perfectly capable of making two hot drinks, Mr Wight asked Mackenzie how her journey had been.

'You could've got a taxi or a helicopter. Why'd you take the train?' Mr Wight questioned when his granddaughter told him she was tired from her long rail journey.

'Turning up in a helicopter or some fancy cab having come from a city hundreds of miles away would kind of give the game away. In case you've forgotten, no-one is supposed to know. Besides, I'm not a princess. The train is perfectly good enough for me,' Mackenzie replied.

Mr Wight hadn't forgotten about the thing that Mackenzie was referring to, nor had he thought she was a princess. He had simply made a daft suggestion. As he didn't know what one did after making a daft suggestion, he decided to swiftly move the conversation on.

'Have you any plans for your time here? I don't know personally, but I have heard that there's a decent nightlife here. There's many daytime things to do too,' Mr Wight enquired.

'I'm not sure. I don't know how to know what to do with myself. It definitely won't have anything to do with the nightlife though. Going out drinking really isn't my thing,' Mackenzie told her grandad.

'It's difficult to know what to do in a new town, isn't it? Took me a while to adjust when I came down here. I'm sure you'll find your feet here,' Mr Wight said.

'I suppose,' Mackenzie replied.

Something about the tone in which Mackenzie answered seemed to suck the energy out of the room. Mr Wight wondered if she was missing the family she'd left at home.

'Drinking isn't my thing either. Tea is good for me,' Mr Wight said, holding up his mug.

Mackenzie didn't reply.

Knowing his tea was getting cold, Mr Wight downed the last of it. As he drank, he thought of how nice it had been to make his tea in a spotless mug from a sparkling kitchen. Thinking of the person who'd cleaned the kitchen gave him an idea.

Chapter Three

As she parked her boyfriend's Dacia Duster outside Mr Wight's flower-adorned cottage, Emma-Leigh wondered if Mackenzie would be home, like she had been a week ago.

Just in case Mackenzie *was* home, Emma-Leigh knocked on the door. It was swiftly opened by Mackenzie's grandad.

'Hello, young Miss Layton! In case you're wondering, I'm home deliberately to see you. There's something I want to talk to you about,' Mr Wight cried when he saw Emma-Leigh, who was unmarried and had Layton for a surname.

'Is something wrong with my cleaning?' Emma-Leigh asked.

'Wrong? Perish the thought! Your cleaning is perfect, and it's not what I want to talk about anyway. My enquiry isn't strictly professional,' Mr Wight replied.

The idea of an enquiry that wasn't strictly professional made Emma-Leigh uneasy. Mr Wight's words were ambiguous, and their meaning could be very awkward. When she considered the character of the man saying the ambiguous words, she dismissed her discomfort.

'What *is* it about then?' Emma-Leigh asked.

'Mackenzie, who I've sent out for a few bits. She's new to town, and I thought she could do with someone to show her around all the young person things. You're the only young person I know really, so I wondered if you'd mind taking her out someplace,' Mr Wight said.

When she'd met Mackenzie, Emma-Leigh had hoped to make friends with her. It had disappointed her that Mackenzie had been a bit frosty with her. She decided that must be because she'd travelled a long way.

'I'd really like that, if Mackenzie *wants* to be taken out,' Emma-Leigh agreed.

—

While Mackenzie was out shopping, Emma-Leigh managed to clean the upstairs bathroom and dust the rarely-used office. She was pouting while she cleaned a mirror on the landing when Mackenzie appeared behind her, making her jump.

'Grandad asked me to speak to you. Apparently, I made quite an impression on you last week, and you want to show me around town,' Mackenzie told Emma-Leigh.

'Did he?' Emma-Leigh questioned. A second after speaking, she cottoned on. 'Yes, he *did*. *I* asked *him* if I could take *you* out. That's right,' Emma-Leigh lied.

Mackenzie frowned. 'Considering that I was tired and not very chatty, I doubt I made a *good* impression on you,' she said.

'But you did! I really want to take you out. I could show you what we young people do in Colchester,' Emma-Leigh argued.

Much to Emma-Leigh's surprise, Mackenzie started roaring with laughter. The hearty tone of Mackenzie's laugh didn't seem to match her speaking voice or her small size. The contrast was so strange that Emma-Leigh didn't even wonder what she was laughing *about*.

'Grandad *asked* you to show me around town, didn't he?' Mackenzie questioned.

'Yes, he did. I'm a terrible liar,' Emma-Leigh admitted.

'I have no idea if you're a terrible liar. I just know my grandad, and I know that's exactly the sort of thing he'd do,' Mackenzie replied.

Based on the little she knew about Mr Wight, Emma-Leigh *also* thought it was exactly the sort of thing he'd do. It was well-meaning, but ill-judged.

'I was happy to take you out, and I think it would make your grandad happy,' Emma-Leigh said.

'I suppose I'll let you show me around town then. I know very little of this place, so it would be useful, I guess,' Mackenzie agreed.

'You don't *have* to,' Emma-Leigh replied.

Mackenzie shrugged. 'I might as well though. As you say, it'll make Grandad happy,' she said.

Once she'd finished cleaning, Emma-Leigh went out into the garden. Out there she found dead plants, Mr Wight typing on a Sony Vaio laptop, and Mackenzie drawing on an Apple iPad. While Emma-Leigh was trying to work out what the black lines on her iPad screen were, Mackenzie sent it to sleep.

'I'm finished, Mr Wight,' Emma-Leigh announced.

'That's great. Thank you,' Mr Wight replied.

Looking at his granddaughter, Mr Wight asked: 'Have you young ladies made plans?'

'Not yet, but that's okay,' Mackenzie replied.

'*I* have plans. All I need is your number so I can arrange a time with you,' Emma-Leigh said.

'And what are those plans? What are you going to do with me?' Mackenzie asked.

Thinking of her plans made Emma-Leigh's eyes sparkle. 'I'm

going to take you to the best part of Colchester!' she cried, her excitement evident in her voice as well as her eyes.

Chapter Four

The address Emma-Leigh told Mackenzie to meet her at was a contemporary women's fashion boutique. It was on a lane with more pedestrians and fewer cars than the nearby High Street.

'This place is heaven on Earth!' Emma-Leigh cried when Mackenzie found her.

'The shop is called Toothill's, not Heaven on Earth,' Mackenzie pointed out.

'It's the *best* shop, though it has funny staff,' Emma-Leigh told Mackenzie.

Before Mackenzie could question what made the shop the best shop, Emma-Leigh dashed into it. Mackenzie saw no choice but to follow her in.

Behind the counter in the shop was a woman who was examining her nails, which looked real and unbitten. When she heard customers walk into her shop, the woman looked up from her nails and put a smile on her face, which looked fake and cosmetically-enhanced.

'Well, welcome to my shop. I'm Victoria Toothill. How may I assist you?' said the woman with real nails and a fake smile.

Every time shop assistants in clothes shops asked her how they could help, or assist, or whatever wording that particular shop used, Mackenzie was tempted to answer: "By fixing my car." As Mackenzie had neither a car nor a desire to say something she considered to be amusing at that time, she said what everyone said, which was: 'Can you find me some clothes?'

'Well, I'd be surprised if I couldn't, considering that I have a shop full of them. It might take me a while if I don't have the important information I need to make the correct selections. I will obviously need to know your size and what sort of thing you wear,' Victoria replied.

'I think what a woman wears says a lot about her,' Emma-Leigh commented.

It suddenly occurred to Mackenzie that Emma-Leigh was absolutely right. The clothes she picked out on that shopping trip, and their price tags, *would* tell Emma-Leigh a lot about her.

'I'm really not into new contemporary fashion. I tend to buy clothes that are preloved and were fashionable a long time ago,' Mackenzie told Emma-Leigh and Victoria.

Victoria pursed her lips. 'Well, all our clothes are very much *in* fashion now and in perfect condition. We *do* do nice dresses that you could wear if you ever wished to dress up properly,' she said.

'Are you suggesting wearing preloved old-fashioned clothes *isn't* dressing up properly? Are you the expert in what counts as dressing properly?' Mackenzie questioned with her hands on her hips.

'Well, you know what I mean,' Victoria replied.

'Oh yes. I know exactly what you mean,' Mackenzie confirmed.

When Mackenzie folded her arms, Emma-Leigh decided it would be a good idea for them to leave the shop.

Evidently, Victoria felt the same as Emma-Leigh, for she said: 'If our style doesn't suit you, I'm sure there are a few specialist places that stock clothes for people like you.'

'Fine by me,' Mackenzie replied.

Without a word to Emma-Leigh, Mackenzie stormed out the door.

'I guess she doesn't like our stock,' Victoria said with a shrug.

'If she's anything like me, it's not the *stock* she disliked,' Emma-Leigh replied.

Victoria raised an eyebrow, as if she expected Emma-Leigh to explain herself. She didn't get an explanation, for Emma-Leigh followed Mackenzie out of the shop.

'When you said the staff were funny, I didn't think you meant they judged you for your style! Who does she think she is?' Mackenzie ranted at Emma-Leigh when she joined her on the bustling pavement.

'That wasn't who I was talking about. When *I* go in, it's usually a chaotic but talented woman who's about our age. I rarely see *that* woman,' Emma-Leigh replied.

'Thank goodness! You wouldn't *want* to see her!' Mackenzie cried.

The passionate *dislike* Mackenzie had for Victoria of Toothill's made Emma-Leigh passionately *like* Mackenzie. She admired women who showed strong feelings.

'If you're always as fiery as that, I think we're going to get on,' Emma-Leigh said.

Mackenzie frowned. 'I was just saying what I thought. Maybe I was a bit too strong,' she told Emma-Leigh.

Standing on the pavement near Toothill's, Mackenzie had forgotten that she was in many people's way. As town dwellers, those people were used to having their path blocked, so they just swarmed round Mackenzie.

'I *liked* it! You weren't exactly rude. You were just forthright.

There are too many meek and mild people in this world, and you're so not one of them,' Emma-Leigh enthused.

'*You're right about that,*' Mackenzie thought. 'I just say what I think, though I don't tend to get emotional. I am usually nice. Shopping has probably unsettled me,' Mackenzie said out loud.

'*How can shopping unsettle you? That's the opposite of what shopping does!*' Emma-Leigh thought. Out loud, Emma-Leigh asked: 'Don't you like shopping?'

Judging by the look on Emma-Leigh's face, if Mackenzie told her she hated shopping, she'd take it as a personal insult. As Mackenzie *didn't* hate shopping, and she didn't want to upset Emma-Leigh, she said: 'I get worried that I'm going to overspend.'

Only then did it occur to Emma-Leigh that she hadn't asked Mackenzie if she had the money to shop. She'd assumed, as she was living with her grandad and probably paying minimal rent, if any, that Mackenzie had plenty of spare cash. It now seemed like her assumption had been wrong.

'I should have thought of that. It's easy to do, I know,' Emma-Leigh murmured.

The shop-lined Lanes of Colchester were full of people and vehicles, all making noise, so Mackenzie didn't hear Emma-Leigh.

'We can shop if you want to though. I get that this is what you like doing in Colchester,' Mackenzie told Emma-Leigh.

Emma-Leigh shook her head. 'No, I have a better idea. I'm going to take you somewhere cheap and cheerful,' she replied.

While following Emma-Leigh out of the town centre to the cheap and cheerful place, Mackenzie spotted a shop she'd love to shop in, if only she could justify the amount of money she'd inevitably blow there.

'Everything alright? We don't have to go to the place I've got in mind,' Emma-Leigh said.

It was that that made Mackenzie realise she'd stopped dead to gaze longingly at the shop with rails just inside the window full of clothes that were older than her.

'I'm fine, thank you. I was just wondering; wondering about where you might be taking me,' Mackenzie replied.

'Nowhere special, but it's fun, and relatively inexpensive,' Emma-Leigh told Mackenzie.

Leaving the shop she liked the look of so much behind, Mackenzie followed Emma-Leigh to the cheap and cheerful place that wasn't special, but was fun and relatively inexpensive.

5

Chapter Five

'Ooh, a snooker club. How did you know?' Mackenzie asked Emma-Leigh when she saw the sign outside The Colneside Entertainment Centre, which Emma-Leigh had taken her to.

The sign outside The Colneside Entertainment Centre told readers that the vast rectangle of concrete was home to an arcade, a bowling alley, a snooker club, karaoke pods, a steakhouse, and a coffee shop. The appearance of the people hanging around by the sign suggested to Mackenzie that all the things listed on the sign were relatively inexpensive.

Instead of admitting she'd had no idea Mackenzie liked snooker, and that she had intended for them to bowl, Emma-Leigh said: 'I guessed.'

A tired, carpeted, multi-flight staircase took Mackenzie and Emma-Leigh up to the snooker club. Though it was somewhere she'd never been before, the sound of cues striking Phenolic resin balls made the bar area of the snooker club seem familiar to Mackenzie.

As she *had* been there before, the bar area of the snooker club, with its one rarely-used dartboard, one large TV showing sport, two bored barmen, and seven pool tables, *was* familiar to Emma-Leigh.

'We certainly *do* have a table free for you. We have five in the main room, in fact, and both the special ones in rooms of their own. There's just one guy in, practicing by himself,' one of the barmen told Emma-Leigh when asked if she and her friend could have a table for two hours.

With this knowledge and a tray of snooker balls, Mackenzie and Emma-Leigh made their way to the main snooker room off of the bar area.

Just as the bored barmen had said, there was one man in the snooker room. The one man looked up from his game and said: 'Hello, Emma-Leigh and whoever you've got with you.'

'Hi, Morton,' Emma-Leigh replied. Turning to Mackenzie, Emma-Leigh said: 'Mackenzie, this is Morton. He's my friend's boyfriend's friend. Morton, meet Mackenzie. She's my favourite client's granddaughter.'

'Nice to meet you,' Mackenzie and Morton said in unison.

Emma-Leigh looked from Mackenzie to Morton, and from Morton to Mackenzie. For the first time since meeting Morton a year ago, she wondered if he was looking for a relationship. She simultaneously wondered if *Mackenzie* was looking for a relationship.

When she looked down at her hands, Emma-Leigh realised all she was carrying was a tray of snooker balls. 'I forgot drinks. Why don't I leave you here with Morton and the balls so you can set up?' she suggested.

'Doesn't "Morton and the balls" sound like a band? A band that would have a committed fan base, but would never appear in the Official Singles Chart Top one-hundred?' Morton said, using his fingers for quotation marks.

As Emma-Leigh had spoken first, Mackenzie answered her first. 'Do get drinks, if you don't mind. I'll have a lemonade,' she told her.

'Are you sure you don't want alcohol? I'll be here for hours, and I don't get any more entertaining,' Morton questioned with a smile.

'I am very sure, and "Morton and the balls" *does* sound like an alternative band,' Mackenzie replied, mirroring Morton's smile and his use of fingers for quotation marks.

Now that she had Mackenzie's drink order, and Morton had made an amusing remark, Emma-Leigh returned to the bar area, leaving a tray of snooker balls behind.

With practiced ease, Mackenzie removed the twenty-two balls from the specially-moulded plastic tray Emma-Leigh had been handed them in, and rolled them all over the table. She placed the red ones in the wooden triangle provided, the white one at the bottom of the table, and the other ones on the white spots marked for them on the green baize.

As Mackenzie finished setting up her table before Emma-Leigh returned with their drinks, she watched Morton play. He strutted around the table as if there was no-one else in the room. When he got down on a shot and, with a perfectly-struck cue ball, made a red ball eight feet away from him roll into a pocket, Mackenzie understood why he walked with such confidence. '*He's almost as good as me*,' Mackenzie thought to herself.

The next few shots Morton attempted were all ambitious, all successful, and all entertained Mackenzie.

'They were chatting amongst themselves and took ages to notice me! Can you believe it?!' Emma-Leigh cried as she came clomping back into the room with drinks just as Morton was playing a thin cut, a shot that requires precision and absolute concentration.

Distracted by Emma-Leigh's entrance, Morton missed the thin cut.

'It happens a lot down here,' Mackenzie replied.

'"Down here"? Are you a Northerner? You don't sound like one, but that comment suggests that you are,' Morton asked.

In her head, but not in reality, Mackenzie kicked herself. 'Yes, I'm a Northerner, but I have a brain, I shower every morning, I don't have a whippet, and I'm not friendly,' she told Morton.

'Is that not true of most Northerners?' Morton questioned.

Emma-Leigh chortled. 'It's a stereotype, Morton. A stereotype that Mackenzie is saying she doesn't fit with,' she explained.

'I know that, thank you. It seems you misunderstood. I was saying I thought very few people matched the Northerner stereotype,' Morton replied.

When Emma-Leigh didn't answer him, Morton turned his attention back to his almost-empty snooker table.

On the wall of the snooker room were racks with cues in. The cues were in varying conditions, weights, and lengths. Mackenzie examined them carefully before removing a well-used short and light cue with a domed tip. Emma-Leigh took a long cue that had pink and purple detailing on it and a worn-down flat tip.

With an intense look on her face, Emma-Leigh strolled up to the bottom of the snooker table, where the white cue ball was waiting for her. Using her battered and unwieldy, but pretty, cue, she wacked the white ball into the triangle of red balls, scattering them all over the top end of the table.

On her way to the snooker table from the wall she'd been leaning on, Mackenzie picked out three reds that she could pot. Two of them, she could pot and leave the cue ball in position to pot a colour. This was handy, as in the game of snooker, the aim is to pot a red, which once potted stays off the table, and a colour (in snooker, red doesn't count as a colour, but black does), which gets replaced. If there are no reds, the aim is to pot the colours in ascending order according to how many points they're worth. To some people, though not Mackenzie and Morton, the aim of snooker is to hit any ball you can and enjoy doing it.

Once at the table, Mackenzie used the cue she'd picked up from the wall to tap the white ball so it gently encouraged a red ball to fall into the pocket. Potting the red allowed Mackenzie to make the cue ball force the black ball into another pocket.

'You're good at this, aren't you?' Emma-Leigh said.

'I've been playing since I was seven,' Mackenzie replied without taking her eye off the red ball six feet away from her that she intended to send off the table through the middle pocket.

By the time it was Emma-Leigh's turn again, she was forty-eight points behind. She was engrossed by comments on her latest profile picture, so unaware she was allowed to play again.

'Have you given up? There's still more than enough on the table to beat me,' Mackenzie told Emma-Leigh.

'Oh, I was looking at something on my phone. I haven't given up yet, not at all,' Emma-Leigh replied.

'Perhaps you should,' Morton murmured.

Emma-Leigh glared at Morton. 'What did you say?' she asked.

Thinking that Emma-Leigh simply hadn't heard him, Morton repeated: 'Perhaps you should give up.'

'Why? Mackenzie said I still have a chance,' Emma-Leigh questioned, folding her arms.

'No, Mackenzie said there are more than enough points on the table to beat her. That's a different thing. Just because there are points available, doesn't mean you will get them. Despite my best efforts to improve your game, it is highly unlikely you can win this frame,' Morton corrected.

Whilst she was trying to think of a good response, Emma-Leigh's phone, which was still in her hand, buzzed loudly. In lieu of answering Morton, she read the WhatsApp message that had just come through.

'Ah, it's my Ronnie! He's home early and asks when I'll be back,' Emma-Leigh announced.

Even though she suspected she already knew the answer, Mackenzie asked: 'Who's Ronnie?'

'My man,' Emma-Leigh replied while typing out a reply to her man.

That was the answer Mackenzie had expected. She considered asking how long they'd been together, but as she didn't care about the answer, she didn't.

'I should be with *him* really. Can I cut this short and make up for it another time?' Emma-Leigh asked.

'Go on then. If I had a man, I'd probably want to be with him,' Mackenzie replied.

A deep frown appeared on Emma-Leigh's face, which confused Mackenzie, as she'd just given her what she wanted. 'You don't have a man?' Emma-Leigh questioned.

'No,' Mackenzie told Emma-Leigh, wondering why it mattered.

Snapping her phone case shut, Emma-Leigh said: 'I'll soon fix that.'

Before Mackenzie could tell Emma-Leigh that it wasn't a problem and it didn't need fixing, Emma-Leigh said goodbye and skipped out of the room.

'Shame. I was enjoying playing snooker,' Mackenzie muttered to herself as the door slammed shut in Emma-Leigh's wake.

'I'm still here, playing snooker, and my two hours have almost run out. We could play against each other, if you wish to,' Morton said.

Mackenzie had forgotten Morton was present. She span round to face him. 'Sounds good to me,' she told him.

Morton shuffled on the spot. 'I wasn't being serious,' he replied.

'Why not? Afraid of being beaten by a girl?' Mackenzie asked with a smile.

'No. No-one of any gender beats me, at least not regularly. I'm afraid of boring a girl to death, not being beaten by her,' Morton explained.

The smile on Mackenzie's face grew wider. She clutched the cue she was using as if it was a mighty spear. 'Now *that* sounds like a challenge, and there's nothing boring about a challenge! Bring it on!' she cried.

6

Chapter Six

When she tiptoed into the lounge at gone 10pm, Mackenzie expected to have the room to herself. When she found the light on and Mr Wight in his tatty winged armchair with his laptop in front of him, she almost jumped.

'I heard a car. Did you get yourself a taxi?' Mr Wight asked his granddaughter.

As she was so surprised to see him, Mackenzie didn't really hear Mr Wight's question. 'What are you doing up?!' she asked him.

'Supping tea and hunting for bargains, that's what I'm doing,' Mr Wight replied.

'At ten o'clock at night?' Mackenzie questioned.

'Yes, unless the clock in the corner's wrong,' Mr Wight confirmed.

While tittering out of politeness at her grandad's somewhat amusing remark, Mackenzie hung her Atmosphere duffle coat on the oak hat stand in the corner of the lounge.

'So, what have you been up to?' Mr Wight asked.

Next to the hat stand was a rocking chair in a similar style, which

Mackenzie sat in to tell Mr Wight about her day. 'Emma-Leigh took me shopping, but I didn't buy anything, for obvious reasons,' Mackenzie replied.

'You say obvious, but I can't think of them. Buying yourself a nice dress is hardly going to make people think you've done well for yourself,' Mr Wight said.

'It would if the dress was a vintage designer piece. Also, I don't think you can say I've *done* well for myself. I didn't earn that money,' Mackenzie replied.

Mr Wight sighed and shut his laptop. 'When I said you've done well for yourself, it wasn't just money I was talking about. It doesn't matter that you didn't work for that money. It's still yours, and you can do with it what you wish, no matter what anyone tells you,' he told Mackenzie.

As Mackenzie *did* know the money Mr Wight was referring to was hers to do what she wished with, she nodded. 'As that's the case, shouldn't you stop telling me what to do with it?' she questioned.

'I haven't told you what to do with it. I can't stop doing something I never started doing,' Mr Wight replied.

'True. You win that one,' Mackenzie conceded.

Mr Wight chuckled. 'You remind me of your grandmother so much sometimes,' he said. It was only when Mackenzie frowned that it occurred to Mr Wight she might not have taken his words as the compliment they were meant to be. 'The best bits of her, when she'd have been around your age,' he explained.

Like most of her family, Mackenzie didn't know how to talk to her grandad about her grandmother. She wasn't sure what to *think* of her grandmother, let alone what to *say* about her to the man who was married to her for over forty years.

Late at night, when none of the occupants spoke, Mr Wight's cottage was almost silent. All that could be heard was the ticking of the grandfather clock in the opposite corner to the hat stand. Less than a fortnight ago, Mackenzie had lived somewhere where silence was non-existent. Something or someone was always making noise. It was so normal that Mackenzie had learnt to tune it out. Having no noise to tune out unsettled Mackenzie almost as much as the mention of her grandmother.

When she remembered the first question her grandad had asked her when she'd entered the lounge, Mackenzie blurted out: 'I *did* get a taxi. It came just a couple of minutes after I called it, and the driver barely said two words to me.'

'Oh, you did then? That's good. Where'd it take you from? What'd you been up to?' Mr Wight asked. His eagerness to hear about what Mackenzie had done with her day was evident in his voice.

'It took me from this sort of family entertainment place. You know the sort of place you find on some industrial estates with bowling, arcades, and that?' Mackenzie replied.

'I know the type of place you mean. Did you play on the penny pushers then? You used to love them in Scarborough,' Mr Wight asked.

Pleasant memories of her seaside holidays with her grandad and grandmother played in Mackenzie's head as if they were scenes in an immersive film. She knew the memories weren't accurate, for in them the sky was a glorious blue and not full of seagulls trying to nick her chips, but that didn't matter to her. What mattered was that they made her almost as happy as she'd been at the time. They also made her forget she was in the middle of a conversation.

'I meant two penny machines, and I suppose that as you're older now, you probably didn't,' Mr Wight said.

'I played *snooker*, but thinking about it, it's quite possible that Emma-Leigh meant for us to play the arcades or bowling,' Mackenzie told Mr Wight.

The mention of snooker made Mr Wight's blue eyes sparkle.

'Snooker? Poor Miss Layton. I bet she didn't know she was in the company of the next Reanne Evans,' he replied.

'As good as I am, I don't think I could win the World Championship twelve times. Emma-Leigh *plainly* couldn't. She doesn't even strike the ball properly,' Mackenzie answered.

Mr Wight frowned, and his eyes dimmed. 'Oh, so you didn't get a decent match then? That's a shame,' he said.

'*Emma-Leigh* didn't give us a decent match, bless her, but there was a lad she knew on the table next to us. Emma-Leigh had to go to her fella, so I ended up playing that lad. He was actually pretty good. We spent a lot of time trying to outfox each other. The hours flew by,' Mackenzie replied.

'He *must* be good to give *you* a game. Was he a nice lad?' Mr Wight asked.

'He was a *quiet* lad,' Mackenzie replied.

'All the best lads are,' Mr Wight commented wistfully.

One of the things Mr Wight had noticed when he'd moved from Yorkshire to Essex was how loud everyone was. A while later, he had noticed how long everyone talked for. To him, in Essex, loud and lengthy seemed to be the default setting for all conversations, especially those involving young men. He didn't like it very much, so he was glad to hear that the man Mackenzie had played with wasn't like most of the young men he saw.

For the first time, it occurred to Mr Wight that, as Mackenzie was now living in Essex, she'd probably end up dating someone local. That someone could be like the majority of young men he saw. A few seconds later, it occurred to him that the man Mackenzie had played snooker with was probably local, and might be single.

'It was such a lovely night. Because Morton barely said two words, I could be myself, which was great,' Mackenzie said, thinking about the local and probably single man that she'd played snooker with.

Something about what Mackenzie said confused Mr Wight. 'Can't you be yourself with chatty people?' he questioned.

'Well, no, because if I have to talk to them, then sooner or later I show myself for who I am,' Mackenzie replied.

That didn't help Mr Wight understand. 'You do, but why is that a problem?' he asked.

'People like me don't get on well in this world. I've moved to a new town, so I thought I may as well become a different person for a new and easier life,' Mackenzie explained.

Mr Wight shook his head. 'One of the things I don't understand about this world is the whole becoming a different person malarkey. I've met all sorts of people in my life, and I'm afraid to say I didn't quite like some of them, but I'd not expect them to become different people. If you're you, you're *you*, and that's that. All you *can* be is you, whoever that is. Being someone else should be something only actors do,' he said.

Mackenzie raised an eyebrow. 'You're wrong. There are so many circumstances that I can think of where it's a good thing to be a different person. Dreadful people *ought* to become different people, and for decent people like us, changing yourself can simply be fun or it can help you get through life. I don't see anything wrong with behaving a bit differently for an easier life,' she argued.

A healthy debate, such as the one he found himself in with Mackenzie, amused Mr Wight. He enjoyed being challenged, and delighted in coming up with a good argument, even if it took him a while.

'I'm gonna pop to bed now. Sleep will help me convince you that you should be yourself,' Mr Wight said.

Following her grandad up his steep stairs, Mackenzie replied: 'I wish you were right, but certain people, like myself, can't be ourselves in this world.'

Chapter Seven

'I have to ask you a question now that shows just how early into our friendship we are,' Emma-Leigh said to Mackenzie as together, they entered a venue called On the Way Home.

'What's that?' Mackenzie asked.

'I said: "I'm going to ask a question now that shows our friendship is in its early stages",' Emma-Leigh told Mackenzie.

'I heard, just about. I meant: "What is the question?",' Mackenzie replied.

Whilst waiting to find out what this question was that showed how early into her friendship with Emma-Leigh she was, Mackenzie had walked with her to the bar. Behind it stood a man wearing fuchsia trousers and waistcoat that contrasted with his lemon-yellow shirt and the matte black wall behind him.

'What's your tipple?' the man in brightly-coloured clothing asked.

Emma-Leigh clicked her fingers. '*That's* the question!' she cried.

'Yes, it is the question. This is a drinking establishment, after all. If you don't drink, we're just an establishment, and to me, "establishment" doesn't scream fun. It doesn't even *whisper* fun,' the man in brightly-coloured clothing replied.

Because the barman had misunderstood her, Emma-Leigh chortled. 'That's perfectly true, but I was referring to a conversation I was having with Mackenzie. I think it says something about your friendship with someone if you don't know what they drink. In *our* case, it says I haven't known Mackenzie long,' Emma-Leigh told the barman.

'Ah, I see. This should be quite revealing then. You're about to learn a lot about Mackenzie,' the barman said.

'What's revealing about what I drink?' Mackenzie questioned.

The barman paused to consider this. 'Quite a bit, as it happens. If you drink vodka, then all you care about is getting drunk, because it tastes of nothing much. If you drink *lager*, you're drinking for the sake of drinking. Honestly, who *likes* lager? Every drink says something about its drinkers,' he replied.

Gazing longingly down the bar at the few beer pumps, Mackenzie wondered what bitter said about its drinkers.

Over the barman's shoulder was a list of drinks so long that Mackenzie knew she couldn't read all of them. She focused her attention on one particular bit of the list that she thought said: "Trendy, but not knowledgeable".

'Gordon's Premium Pink and Fever Tree Premium Indian Tonic Water for me,' Mackenzie told the barman and Emma-Leigh.

A glance at the smile on Emma-Leigh's face told Mackenzie she'd made the right choice.

'I'm usually a white wine girl, but that sounds good to me. I've heard a lot about pink gin, but haven't tried it yet. I think tonight's the night to rectify that,' Emma-Leigh said.

'Cool. Two all the rage G and T's coming up,' the barman replied.

Once Emma-Leigh had paid for their all the rage gin and tonics, she and Mackenzie took a small table in one corner from which they could see the entrance, the bar, and the DJ.

'How was Ronald?' Mackenzie asked Emma-Leigh after a sip of her gin and tonic.

Emma-Leigh chortled. '*Ronnie*, you mean? I only call him Ronald when I'm cross with him,' she replied.

'Sorry. How was *Ronnie*?' Mackenzie corrected.

'Let's just say I'm glad I went home, and I certainly *wasn't* cross with him that night,' Emma-Leigh told Mackenzie.

'Why were you cross with him? What had he done?' Mackenzie questioned.

'I *wasn't* cross with him. I was anything *but* cross with him by the early hours of that morning. That's why I'm so glad I went home,' Emma-Leigh said.

It was at this moment that the drum and base track playing over the bar's sound system reached its repetitive crescendo of a chorus. Rather than compete with the extensive network of speakers, Mackenzie sipped her gin and tonic. She didn't tell Emma-Leigh that she hated the bittersweet taste, but the grimace on her face did.

Across the table from Mackenzie, Emma-Leigh was sipping *her* drink. She considered talking about how much she disliked it, but decided against that when another idea popped into her head.

'Did you say you don't have a man?' Emma-Leigh asked.

'No, I *do* have a mum. She still lives Up North though,' Mackenzie replied.

'Oh, so you left a boyfriend behind in Sheffield?' Emma-Leigh questioned.

The mention of a boyfriend in Sheffield made Mackenzie wonder what her grandad had told Emma-Leigh. It seemed unlikely to her that he'd talked about her ex-boyfriend, but she couldn't think of any other explanation for Emma-Leigh knowing she'd left someone in the city she still thought of as home. It also confused her, because it had nothing to do with the last thing she thought Emma-Leigh had said.

'I did, but what's that got to do with my mum?' Mackenzie asked.

'Your mum? What's your mum got to do with *anything*? I thought we were talking about *men*, not *mums*,' Emma-Leigh replied.

Realisation dawned on Mackenzie. 'I misheard you, and I think *you* misheard *me*. Given how loud it is in here, that's no surprise,' she explained.

Determined not to let an overly-loud DJ get in the way of potential matchmaking, Emma-Leigh pressed on.

'So, *did* you leave someone behind in Sheffield? Are you single?' Emma-Leigh asked.

'My ex cheated on me. That's one of the reasons why I moved down here,' Mackenzie replied.

Emma-Leigh gasped. 'Oh, that's awful! Good to give yourself space though, so you can consider if your relationship has a future,' she said.

Thinking Emma-Leigh had misheard yet again, Mackenzie repeated: 'My ex *cheated* on me.'

'Yes, you said. That's why *I* said about it being good to get away so you can think about what's next for you and him,' Emma-Leigh replied.

'*Nothing* is next for us. We *have* no future. He *cheated* on me,' Mackenzie told Emma-Leigh.

Just as the DJ segued from one track to another, Emma-Leigh frowned. Mackenzie wondered if she didn't like the song.

'Yes, I heard the first and second times. Your ex-boyfriend cheated on you, which is awful,' Emma-Leigh said.

'If you heard, why did you think my ex and I have a future? What self-respecting woman stays with a man who isn't faithful?' Mackenzie asked.

'My Ronnie cheated on me twice and I certainly have self respect, so *I'm* the answer to your question,' Emma-Leigh replied.

'What? But they never stop! Haven't you heard the phrase: "Once a cheater, always a cheater?",' Mackenzie blurted out.

In one second flat, Emma-Leigh's whole demeanour changed. She folded her arms and narrowed her eyes. 'Haven't *you* heard that that phrase isn't true?!' Emma-Leigh snapped.

'No, because it *is* true! These men have no respect for women, and they don't suddenly get it! They never truly get caught out, so they just carry on. If you stay with someone like that, you know you'll never be their one and only,' Mackenzie retorted.

Emma-Leigh shrieked shrilly. 'How *dare* you say that about my Ronnie? Yes, he's had a couple of dalliances, but we've been together for six years. That's par for the course. The first one was weeks after we got together, and after the second, he promised me I'd never find him in bed with another woman again. I always knew he had a rep, and he deserved it too, but not anymore. The version of myself I am today is more than good enough for him. He'll *never* be unfaithful again, no matter what your stupid sayings say,' she roared.

Worried that Emma-Leigh might burst a blood vessel through pure rage, Mackenzie said: 'I apologise. I shouldn't have said what I said. Your Ronnie must be very different to Shaun.'

'You *should* be sorry!' Emma-Leigh replied.

Mackenzie had hoped her apology would calm Emma-Leigh, but there was no sign it had. She saw no point in staying with Emma-Leigh when she was so angry with her.

'I'm going to the ladies. If you can't get past the fact I offended you, you know where the door is. I'll understand if you're not here when I get back,' Mackenzie said.

As she walked away from the table, Mackenzie could feel Emma-Leigh's gaze burning into her. When she got to the cool and calm ladies loos, she breathed a huge sigh of relief. She hadn't expected to have a row, nor had she expected to have to think about Shaun, the man who'd shocked her and rocked her trust in people.

8

Chapter Eight

When she returned to the main bar of On the Way Home from its ladies loo, Mackenzie saw that Emma-Leigh was still sat at their table. '*She's calmed down then,*' she thought to herself. A second later, Mackenzie thought: '*Oh, I can hear myself think. The DJ's gone then.*'

Because she was looking at her phone, Emma-Leigh didn't see Mackenzie until she sat down across from her.

'Just a second,' Emma-Leigh murmured, still looking at her phone.

While waiting for Emma-Leigh, Mackenzie picked up her drink. She swiftly put it down again when she remembered that she'd left it unattended and she hadn't liked it anyway.

'Right, I'm with you now. Thanks for coming back,' Emma-Leigh said, snapping her phone case shut.

'I wanted to see if you'd calmed down,' Mackenzie replied.

'I have. As soon as you walked out, I thought about how I felt when I found out Ronnie had cheated for the second time. Had someone have spoken to me back then, I would have been like you. I wouldn't have appreciated someone like me going on about a future with a man who, at that time, I hated. You did well not to slap me,' Emma-Leigh told Mackenzie.

After a moment's consideration, Mackenzie decided against admitting that she had been tempted to slap Emma-Leigh.

Instead of telling Emma-Leigh how much she'd irritated her, Mackenzie decided to ask about how it had felt to be cheated on. Never before had she met someone who she knew had experienced it.

'Did you get angry then? Was that how you felt?' Mackenzie questioned.

'Eventually, but that took a while. I made the mistake of assuming there must be a reason for what he'd done, and I thought *I* was the reason. The mirror was not my friend back then. At some point, I went from being cross with myself for messing up somehow to being cross with *him* for making me feel so bad. That, thank goodness, faded into a more mature understanding that I'm not responsible for what he did, but I could have done more. Now I *am* doing more, and we're together again. I'm even starting to trust him again. I don't feel the need to know where he is anymore,' Emma-Leigh replied.

To Mackenzie, there was something disappointingly unfamiliar about the feelings Emma-Leigh described.

'*I* don't feel angry or like it's my fault. I feel *stupid*, for not knowing sooner, but I don't feel at fault for what he did. I just wonder how I didn't see it. I wasn't the only one though. When I had to admit to my family what had happened, they were shocked. My mum was so shocked that she questioned if I was even right. He seemed like such a nice man, it didn't seem possible that he'd done something so despicable,' Mackenzie revealed.

'*You* feel stupid? Imagine how I felt. Ronnie *did* have a reputation. People who knew him used to joke about how many beds he could sleep in in one week. I thought it was *just* a joke though. He always used to laugh about it, even when we were together. It never occurred to me that it was actually true. It should have done, but it didn't. If I can trust a man whose friends made it quite clear what sort of man he was, no wonder you trusted someone who seemed *nice*,' Emma-Leigh told Mackenzie.

'Is anyone *truly* nice? Is there a man out there worthy of trust? I had *thoughts* about other men when I was with Shaun. It wouldn't have taken much for me to act on them, and then *I* wouldn't have deserved someone's trust. For all we know, *everyone* cheats,' Mackenzie questioned.

Deciding that she needed more alcohol before she answered Mackenzie, Emma-Leigh downed the last of her pink gin and tonic. She'd forgotten that she hated the taste, and made a funny noise as she gulped it down.

'I remember thinking that, but there *are* nice men out there. I know that now. My friend fell in love with one last year, and now, thanks to a great deal of work on my part, my Ronnie is one too. He admitted his mistakes and became a different man. A man I can trust and love, who respects me,' Emma-Leigh assured Mackenzie.

'But how *can* you be sure? How can you trust him?' Mackenzie asked.

'Because, Mackenzie, I love him, and he loves me. He knows what he did to me was wrong. It hurts him almost as much as it hurts me to think of it. We're past that now. We're different people. Having done it twice, and seen the damage it did to me, I know he'll never do it again,' Emma-Leigh replied.

When Mackenzie didn't answer, Emma-Leigh said: 'That's why I said you and Shaun might have a future. If you make it clear that he hurt you and it's up to him to change and win you back, then you're sorted.'

'But he *won't* admit it! He got cross with me for accusing him, and completely denied it. He asked what on Earth had made me question him. I didn't tell him, because it might help him hide it from others in future. I just told him that how I knew was irrelevant. All that mattered was that he'd done something despicable, he'd broken my heart, and I never wanted to see him again,' Mackenzie replied.

It surprised Emma-Leigh that Mackenzie's Shaun had asked what had made Mackenzie think he'd cheated when he denied doing it. If Shaun *had* cheated, it seemed like a very bold move to ask for evidence. Her Ronnie had never asked about proof, probably because he knew Emma-Leigh could produce it. She had *chosen* to thrust in his face a phone full of explicit text messages to another woman. It also surprised her that there'd been no sign of trouble with Shaun until Mackenzie had somehow found out that he'd cheated.

Not wanting to ask her relatively-new friend any probing questions, Emma-Leigh declared: 'There *are* good men out there, and I'm going to prove it to you by getting you one.'

'Oh, you are *not* serious! Please don't!' Mackenzie cried.

Emma-Leigh chortled. 'I certainly *am* serious, as you shall see. I helped my friend get with her partner, and I've never seen her so happy. I'm a better matchmaker than the dishy maître d' from *First Dates*, as I shall show you,' she replied.

While Mackenzie was trying to think of a way to convince Emma-Leigh not to match her with someone, a cacophony of indistinct noise erupted from the bar's sound system.

'I can barely hear you, and I didn't like my drink that much. Shall we go?' Mackenzie suggested.

Emma-Leigh nodded her agreement, and the pair got up to leave.

Having spent twenty minutes winding around Colchester in the back of a cab with her, Mackenzie thought Emma-Leigh had forgotten about getting her a man. She was proven wrong when the taxi reached Mr Wight's house and, just before she got out, Emma-Leigh said: 'I *will* find you a nice guy. By the time the weather goes cold, you'll have someone to keep you warm.'

9

Chapter Nine

Having one friend in the area and no job meant that Mackenzie spent a lot of time sitting around in her grandad's house. This meant that, when her mum called her, she had nothing better to do than talk to her.

'Ah, Mackenzie, you picked up. That's good. If you hadn't, I'd have ended up bringing the bin in, and I really don't want to do that in this weather. As you answered, I can leave that until later. I didn't just call to give myself an excuse not to go out in the rain slash sleet. I needed to tell you that I've bought a painting for your dad off eBay,' Mackenzie's mum told her as soon as she answered the call.

'That's nice,' Mackenzie commented.

'You know what eBay is like; some things are Buy Now, and some are auctions that go on forever that end late at night when you want to go to bed. Some things have huge delivery costs on top, some have it included, and some expect you to pick the item up. It's all very confusing,' Mackenzie's mum rambled.

Realising she was going to be on the phone for a while,

Mackenzie walked to the lounge window, from which she could see the neglected back garden.

'Yes, Mum,' Mackenzie said to prompt her mum to continue.

'This painting, which is beautiful by the way, is in some village called Saint Lawrence. It's only twelve miles from you, apparently. I guess being a painting that it's difficult to post, because the seller's made it Collection Only. I didn't realise when I bought it, you see,' Mackenzie's mum went on.

A minute into the phone call, Mackenzie understood the purpose of it. Inside her head, she sighed. Out loud, she said: 'I see.'

There was silence on the line while Mackenzie waited for her mum to ask her to pick up the painting.

'Are you still there, love?' Mackenzie's mum asked.

'Yes,' Mackenzie replied with a smile.

'As it's so close to you, could I ask you to pick up that painting? I'd really appreciate it. You could bring it up here and spend a weekend with us,' Mackenzie's mum asked.

'It's completely possible,' Mackenzie told her mum.

While waiting for her mum to respond, Mackenzie watched a pigeon peck at some weeds on the overgrown lawn.

'Will you come then? We'd love to see you,' Mackenzie's mum asked.

'Yes. I miss Sheffield already, so I'd be happy to come and see you,' Mackenzie confirmed.

'Oh, that's wonderful news! I was up at one in the morning bidding on that thing, and I was worried I was gonna have to let it go. It would've been such a shame. Alf will love it. You are a good'un, Mackenzie,' Mackenzie's mum cried.

After swapping her phone to the other hand, Mackenzie replied: 'I'm glad to be able to help. It's nice to have something to do. I've been so bored.'

Twenty minutes later, after her mum had listed *everything* she'd done in the last three weeks, Mackenzie regretted saying she'd been bored. Though she *said* she was sorry when her mum had to go, she wasn't. She *also* wasn't sorry to have a task to complete and a reason to go back to Sheffield.

Chapter Ten

As soon as Emma-Leigh found out Mackenzie was going to Sheffield for the weekend, she arranged to see her at the Colneside Snooker Club one evening before she left.

When Mackenzie entered what she considered to be the most lifeless building in Colchester and made her way up the stairs to the snooker room, she found Emma-Leigh chatting to two young men.

'I love that she's totally happy for me to come out and do this. I know some girls would give me trouble about spending time with anyone other than her,' one of the men was saying to Emma-Leigh.

The moment Emma-Leigh spotted Mackenzie, she waved her over. 'Mackenzie, hi! Mackenzie, this is Jude, my friend's partner, and Morton, who you met when we came here before. Jude, this is Mackenzie, my client's granddaughter,' she said.

'You were in here, on your own, during the day, Morton?' Jude questioned, more interested in what his friend had got up to than Mackenzie.

'Some numbers didn't crunch, and I needed to ponder what to do about it. This helps me think,' Morton replied.

Emma-Leigh waved her arms emphatically at Mackenzie. 'Hello, didn't you hear me?! This is Mackenzie, who you haven't met before, Jude!' she cried.

The table behind Mackenzie had someone practicing on it, and that someone missed their shot when Emma-Leigh waved. Mackenzie noticed this, and was briefly distracted by a wish to apologise to the person.

'Sorry, Mackenzie. I were just wondering why Morton came here without me. I didn't mean to ignore you. It's nice to meet you,' Jude said.

There was something about Jude, with his curly brown hair and sheepish grin, that made Mackenzie want to smile, so she did.

'It's okay, Jude. Nice to meet you too,' Mackenzie replied.

Having introduced her acquaintances to Mackenzie, Emma-Leigh turned all her attention on her, which allowed Jude and Morton to get back to their game of snooker, which they had abandoned midway through a safety exchange.

'How are you? Are you ready to go up to Sheffield tomorrow?' Emma-Leigh asked Mackenzie.

'I'm worried, because I'm *not* ready. I still don't have a car to get up there, and I can't take the painting on the train. Apart from anything else, this Saint Lawrence place is miles from the nearest station,' Mackenzie replied.

In the few seconds it had taken Emma-Leigh to ask Mackenzie how she was, Morton had potted a long red and a blue, and was working out how to pot more balls. As snooker is a game where players take turns, Jude was standing around waiting, so he heard what Mackenzie said.

'I don't mean to butt in to your conversation, but did I hear you need a car?' Jude asked.

'Yes. I've agreed to pick something up for my mum and take it to her in Sheffield, but I don't have anything to take it up in,' Mackenzie confirmed.

'So is your car with the garage or something?' Jude questioned.

'No, I don't have one. I sold my old one to my friend before I moved down here, and haven't replaced it. I'm so used to having a car that I forgot I don't currently have one,' Mackenzie explained. It then occurred to Mackenzie that it was an odd question for a stranger to ask.

'I just thought that if you don't need it long, and you can insure yourself on it and fill it up, you can have mine. I can walk or borrow my girlfriend's car for a few days, so it don't bother me,' Jude offered before Mackenzie could ask why he was asking about a car.

The kindness of Jude's offer astounded Mackenzie. She didn't even know the man, and he was offering his car to her. She was so astounded that she didn't react how she usually would to offers of help.

'You can *so* tell you're Cecilia's partner. I think some of her generosity has rubbed off you,' Emma-Leigh said to Jude.

'Totally, but how can it not? She's got so *much* helpfulness, some of it's bound to rub off on the people she's with,' Jude agreed.

A slight smile appeared on Emma-Leigh's face, and her hands moved to her hips. 'Is helpfulness a word?' she questioned.

'Depends what dictionary you read, don't it?' Jude replied.

'So, Mackenzie, I think thanks to Jude that you're all sorted,' Emma-Leigh said, turning to her friend.

It didn't escape Mackenzie's notice that Emma-Leigh didn't answer Jude. She didn't comment on it though. There were many things in life that didn't escape her notice that she didn't comment on.

'Yes. Thanks, Jude,' Mackenzie mumbled.

Jude shrugged. 'It don't matter to me. I don't need it,' he said.

On Emma-Leigh and Mackenzie's snooker table, forgotten about by the pair of them, was a black plastic moulded tray of brightly-coloured Phenolic resin balls. The snooker table's green baize bed had six white crosses marked on it for the six colour balls in the tray, and a wooden triangle on the lampshade above it to set up the fifteen red balls.

'Shall I set up the table so we can play?' Mackenzie asked Emma-Leigh.

Emma-Leigh nodded. 'Yes, if you like. I'd have done it, but I've been chatting,' she agreed.

After Mackenzie had set up the balls, without consulting her, Emma-Leigh played the break-off shot to start their game of snooker. People who understand snooker would describe her shot as "aggressive", but as Emma-Leigh *didn't* understand snooker, she had no idea her shot was aggressive.

As Mackenzie *did* understand snooker, she *knew* the shot was aggressive. She also knew it was poor, because even though the cue ball had returned to the baulk end, there were a couple of red balls she could pot. Granted, the reds were nine feet from the white, but that wasn't a problem for Mackenzie. She demonstrated this by making one of the reds bounce along into a corner pocket.

'Wow! She's a match for *you*, Morton!' Jude cried.

'She is. She beat me twice when we played,' Morton agreed.

After a minute of playing on it, Mackenzie was aware of nothing but the snooker table and the balls on it. She didn't see Emma-Leigh leaning on the wall, looking at her phone. She didn't notice Jude repeatedly sliding the marker on the scoreboard that was *on* the wall Emma-Leigh was leaning on.

The table continued to absorb all of Mackenzie's attention until, with thirty-two on the scoreboard that Jude kept updating, the cue ball knocked the blue ball off its spot and stayed there, right in the middle of the table.

'I'm going to need the rest,' Mackenzie mumbled to herself.

'The what?' Emma-Leigh questioned while still looking at her phone.

Pulling the rest out from its hooks under the snooker table, Jude said: 'This. A stick with a metal X on the end.'

Only then did Mackenzie become aware of Jude's presence, and the accurate scoreboard on the wall. 'I could have got that and done the scoreboard myself. You didn't need to do it for me. No-one needs to do anything for me,' Mackenzie pointed out, snatching the rest off of Jude.

'I were just being helpful,' Jude mumbled.

Mackenzie shook her head. 'Sorry, Jude. That didn't come out right,' she told Jude.

'Oh, that's okay then. I thought I'd offended you or something,' Jude replied.

As Jude was going to lend her his car, a huge offer of help that she was grateful for, Mackenzie decided not to tell him that it irritated her when people, especially men, offered her help. Instead, she told him: 'No, of course you didn't offend me. I'm just irritated that I've run out of position.'

'Yeah, that makes sense. What with using the rest, you'll probably miss,' Jude commented.

On the table next to the one on which Mackenzie had run out of position, Morton had also run into a spot of bother. As he'd paused playing to consider his next move, he'd heard Jude's comment to Mackenzie, and replied: 'Based on empirical data, she'll get this.'

'*What* data?' Jude asked.

With the rest Jude had handed her that he'd said she'd miss with, Mackenzie played her shot perfectly. While doing so, she thought: '*Empirical data is basically real-life data.*'

When Morton saw the red Mackenzie had aimed at disappear into the top left pocket, he explained: 'Empirical data is data based on observation and experience, not logic and theory.'

'I've played snooker since I was seven and I've never been taller than this, so there's a lot of empirical data about my ability with the rest. Some of that data comes from my match with Morton, because he kept putting me in difficult positions,' Mackenzie told Jude.

Even though she was looking at her phone, Emma-Leigh had heard what Mackenzie had said, and she snickered at the last bit.

'What?' Jude questioned in reference to the little laugh that escaped Emma-Leigh.

'Nothing,' Emma-Leigh replied with a smile on her face.

As he didn't understand what Emma-Leigh was laughing at, and had worked out how to continue the frame, Morton let himself once again be absorbed by his snooker table and the balls on it.

—

Having overcome the challenge of using the rest, Mackenzie went on to win the frame in one visit.

'Do *I* ever get to play?' Emma-Leigh asked.

Jude nodded at the snooker table he was playing on with Morton, which Morton had nearly cleared. 'I were wondering the same thing. I think if we're to have a chance, you and I should play each other and leave them to do what they do. I somehow think that would be fairer,' he replied.

Distracted by the thought of playing against Mackenzie with his friend watching, Morton missed his shot.

Seeing that Morton has missed, Jude glanced at the scoreboard and said: 'It's obvious I can't come back. You have the frame.'

The thought of playing against Morton again put a smile on Mackenzie's face. 'Do you fancy it?' she asked him.

'Do I fancy what? What is it that you're suggesting?' Morton questioned.

Mackenzie let out a laugh that echoed off the harsh surfaces of the snooker room. 'Taking me on, silly! Are you up for it on this snooker table?' she replied.

Unheard by her friends, a snicker escaped Emma-Leigh.

Morton folded his arms and declared: 'I accept your challenge.'

11

Chapter Eleven

The sound of laughter greeted Mackenzie as she walked round the corner, onto the street that Jude lived on with his partner, Cecilia. The laughter was emanating from a woman with long golden hair soaked with soapy water who was standing with Jude by a Suzuki Swift.

'The water is for the car, not me!' the blonde woman by the car cried.

'There wouldn't *be* any water if you hadn't insisted we clean my car before I give it to her,' Jude pointed out.

'You can't lend someone a dirty car! If you give someone something, it should be in the best condition possible. Besides, it's not just *your* car that's dirty. *My* baby needs attention too after yours,' the blonde woman replied, patting a pale blue Mini Cooper sitting on the driveway she was standing on.

It was at this point that Mackenzie reached the couple, and she decided to make her presence known.

'You *could* have given me a dirty car. It would still have been a big help to me,' Mackenzie told Jude and the blonde woman.

The blonde woman turned to face Mackenzie and smiled. 'You must be Mackenzie. I'm Cecilia, Jude's partner,' she told her.

From the moment she'd turned the corner into Jude's road, Mackenzie had known the wet-and-laughing blonde woman was his partner. Cecilia's demeanour was exactly as Mackenzie had imagined. She didn't *look* how Mackenzie had imagined her though. Cecilia was far tidier and prettier than she'd pictured her.

'Nice to meet you. You have a great boyfriend. I don't know what I'd have done without him,' Mackenzie commented.

The corners of Cecilia's mouth turned up and she gazed at Jude with what looked to Mackenzie like pride in her eyes. 'I *do* have a *wonderful* partner. I bet when you thanked him for the use of his car, he said: "No problem". That's why I love him,' she said.

It wasn't necessary for Cecilia to tell Mackenzie she loved Jude. Mackenzie already knew. She could see it in the way Cecilia looked at him.

The happy atmosphere around Jude and Cecilia meant that Mackenzie couldn't help but mirror their smiles.

For a few moments, the three of them just stood on the pavement outside Jude's house, smiling at each other. The smiles faded when the three of them realised silently staring at each other was uncomfortable.

'Have you got all the rubbish out now?' Cecilia asked Jude.

'Yup. No empty takeaway stuff in the passenger footwell anymore,' Jude confirmed.

To confirm this, Cecilia surreptitiously glanced into Jude's car. She noticed that the footwell was *completely* empty.

'No AA road atlas either. We forgot to put it back,' Cecilia commented.

Jude pretended to slap himself on the forehead. '*I knew* I'd forgot something!' he cried.

The smile Cecilia had had ever since Mackenzie had laid eyes on her grew wider. 'You're most cute when you do that,' she told Jude.

'It's not like I forgot mapbooks often, and I don't get what's cute about it,' Jude replied.

Cecilia tittered. 'You do this thing where you hit your head when you make a mistake. *That's* what I thought was cute,' she explained.

The expression on Jude's face made it quite clear he had no idea he did this thing where he hits his head when he makes a mistake. That was also cute to Cecilia, and it inspired her to give his dumbfounded face an equally-cute peck on the cheek.

The interaction between Jude and Cecilia made it clear to Mackenzie that they'd temporarily forgotten she was there. They were in their own loved-up couple world.

Seeing Jude and Cecilia so entranced by one another reminded Mackenzie of how she and Shaun had been before she'd been told he'd cheated on her. The thought that Shaun may well have been cheating on her for their entire relationship soured the previously-happy memories that Jude and Cecilia brought to Mackenzie's mind.

When Cecilia returned to the real world from her loved-up couple world, she cleared her throat and gazed down at her pointy-toed heeled boots. 'I'll go and get a road atlas,' she murmured, dashing into her house before anyone could answer.

Jude's gaze followed Cecilia into the house. 'Yeah, in case you're wondering, I *do* know how lucky I am,' he commented to Mackenzie once Cecilia was out of sight.

Even the way Jude spoke about Cecilia reminded Mackenzie of Shaun. Shaun had always sung her praises to anyone who'd listen, including Mackenzie herself. He told people time and time again that there was no-one like her, and he was lucky to be the one man who got the one her.

'You look miles away. You okay?' Jude asked Mackenzie.

'*By the end of today, I'll be miles away from here, but miles closer to Shaun,*' Mackenzie thought to herself.

Not wanting to share her thoughts about her Sheffield-dwelling ex-boyfriend, Mackenzie said: 'I was just wondering how long it'll take me to get to Saint Lawrence. It's only twelve miles away, so I'm hoping it won't take long.'

Jude snorted. 'It *ain't*, unless you got a helicopter. There's a great big river between us and there, so it's more like thirty by road. It'll take best part of an hour with traffic and that, and it's down from here, but Sheffield is up, of course,' he informed Mackenzie.

The knowledge that she'd have to travel an hour in the wrong direction rendered Mackenzie speechless.

Before Mackenzie had fully processed the fact that her long drive would be even longer than she'd accounted for, Cecilia came rushing out of her house with a book that could show her exactly how far she'd have to drive.

'No car is complete without a road atlas. Certainly no car going through an unfamiliar area where, thanks to patchy signal, you can't always use your phone to get you out of trouble,' Cecilia told Mackenzie as she placed the aforementioned road atlas into Jude's car's front passenger footwell.

'With or without an atlas, thanks Jude, for lending me your car. I hope you don't mind, Cecilia, that he might have to borrow yours,' Mackenzie said.

The beaming smile on Cecilia's face suggested she didn't mind at all. 'I am most happy that Jude will have to borrow my Mini. It doesn't have a tow bar, which means he can't pull the trailer he needs for his painting and decorating paraphernalia. He forgot this when he offered you the Suzuki,' she told Mackenzie.

'Oh, so I've stopped him working. Sorry,' Mackenzie replied.

'Don't be *sorry*! Jude isn't *supposed* to work weekends, but his boss always makes him. It means I hardly ever get him to myself. This weekend though, he *can't* be made to work, and I can get my work done during the week, so we have a whole weekend together,' Cecilia explained.

Spending a weekend with a beloved partner sounded blissful to Mackenzie. She sighed inside when she thought of what *she'd* be up to that weekend. She withdrew her mental sigh when she thought about the fact that she'd be enduring her mother in *Sheffield*.

'We cleaned the car, we exchanged thanks yous', and we got a mapbook. There ain't anything else, is there?' Jude asked.

'There is! I wanted to ask Mackenzie if she had any trouble with insurance,' Cecilia replied.

'None at all. I just went online and got a temporary policy for three days. I got emailed the certificate, so I didn't even have to wait for the post,' Mackenzie revealed.

Just as Mackenzie had expected her to, Cecilia asked: 'Can I see the certificate?'

As Mackenzie had her phone in her pocket, which she could use to view the certificate she'd been emailed, Cecilia could see the certificate. In just a few seconds, Mackenzie got her phone out and showed it to her.

Satisfied that Mackenzie had suitable insurance, Jude and Cecilia said their goodbyes to her and wished her good luck with her journey.

As she pulled away from their house, Mackenzie watched Jude and Cecilia smile at each other as they washed their blue Mini. The pang of jealousy Mackenzie felt was so strong, it almost physically hurt.

12

Chapter Twelve

The roads the satnav app on Mackenzie's phone sent her down were comfortably wide, but uncomfortably twisty. They crossed miles and miles of countryside with the occasional village along the way. The villages weren't the type you see on postcards with cute cottages and lush communal green spaces. They were just small collections of dependable, but uninspiring, houses, most of which appeared to have been built in the 1970s, along the uncomfortably twisty road.

When Mackenzie passed through one such village, which had two pubs and a pretty church, but no shop, she wondered aloud: 'Why does anyone live here?'

Mackenzie's wonderings did not distract her from the irritating lorry with a boat on its trailer that she'd been stuck behind for the last two miles. As yet, *nothing* had distracted her from the lorry with a boat on its trailer. It was too bothersome to ignore.

As Cecilia had said, the area St Lawrence was in had signal

blackspots. One of those blackspots was around the junction Mackenzie was supposed to turn left at for St Lawrence. Without an internet connection, the satnav app on her phone couldn't function, so it didn't tell her to turn left. As Mackenzie didn't read direction signs, she missed the turning for St Lawrence, and only knew when her phone got signal again and said: 'Perform a U turn where possible.'

The speed limit on the country lane Mackenzie was trundling along was sixty miles an hour, so she felt it wasn't possible at that moment in time to perform the U turn her phone had requested. It was also twisty, so it wasn't safe to overtake the lorry with a boat on its trailer either. All she could do was drive along until she got to another village, where she would then be able to turn around.

The low speed she was traveling at allowed Mackenzie to take in her surroundings. For many miles, all she'd seen apart from the villages, the lorry in front of her, and the road, were fields, and lots of them. To Mackenzie, fields were unimpressive. She knew they were important, but she didn't consider them to be interesting to look at. This meant that she was thoroughly bored, until she noticed light glinting off something in the distance to the left of the road. That something was a river, which was glinting like a glitterball and matched the colour of the sky.

'So *that's* why people live here,' Mackenzie murmured, mesmerised by the bright sunlight shining off the distant river.

Having seen the river, Mackenzie no longer felt cross about it being in her way. In her opinion, it being so pretty excused the travel troubles it caused.

Mackenzie ended up following the lorry with a boat on its trailer all the way to a marina. The marina was just before a village. She assumed that if she drove into that village, she'd find somewhere to turn around.

The village was much smaller than the others Mackenzie had been through, but its architecture was much more varied. A generous-sized house that Mackenzie thought was Georgian caught her eye, as did a more modest 1970s bungalow across the road from it.

After the 1970s bungalow, the road went slightly uphill. Mackenzie followed it, expecting to see more houses, and was surprised when a river greeted her instead. She brought Jude's car to a halt, for she had no choice but to. The road ahead was a slipway straight down into the river. It wasn't possible to drive any further unless she wanted to drown, which she didn't.

At last, Mackenzie had found a suitable spot to turn around, but she didn't perform the manoeuvre immediately. Instead, she turned the engine off so she could sit and stare at the river in front of her. It was the same river she'd seen before, but it looked a lot murkier than it had earlier in the day. She concluded that was just because she was closer to it.

Mackenzie felt her mind drift as she gazed at the river. She felt like it was the sort of place where people might go to think about complicated things.

A minute later, having had enough of looking at the murky river, Mackenzie picked up the road atlas that Cecilia had ensured was in the car. The moment she found the right page, she spotted the turning for St Lawrence that she was now pleased to have missed. She also saw that the river that was blue and sparkly in one place, and murky in another, was called the River Blackwater.

Confident that she'd find it this time, Mackenzie turned Jude's car around and headed for St Lawrence.

—

When Mackenzie saw the painting her mum had ordered for her dad, she thought: *'The murky river looked better than that.'*

'I'm so pleased to have sold it,' the previous owner of the painting told Mackenzie as they handed it to her.

'*I bet you are,*' Mackenzie thought to herself.

'I've always thought it was one of the better examples of my work, you see, and I love that it's found a home that'll love it as much as I loved painting it,' the former painting owner continued.

'*Oh, they painted it. Don't be rude then, Mackenzie,*' Mackenzie told herself in her head.

'My dad will love it,' Mackenzie told the painter of the painting that she had to take to Sheffield.

The painter nodded, as if they were used to their work being praised. Looking at the example of the painter's work in front of her, Mackenzie couldn't imagine that they *were* often praised for their work.

It was then that Mackenzie noticed that the painter's neighbour had left their key in the front door. She pointed it out to the painter.

'Yes, Dorothy's always doing that. I'll pop it through her letter-box in a minute,' the painter said.

The idea of someone leaving their key in the door *once*, let alone *multiple* times, shocked Mackenzie. She had to replay the sentence in her head to be sure she'd heard it right.

'How come she hasn't been burgled?' Mackenzie couldn't help asking.

The painter shrugged. 'Look around you. Does this look like the sort of place where people get burgled?' they asked.

As requested, Mackenzie glanced around herself at the gravel road of tired bungalows.

'Aren't *all* places the sort of places where people get burgled?' Mackenzie questioned.

'No. It occasionally happens here, but it's so rare that it's not worth bothering about. We all look out for each other, so we spot someone up to no good before they can get up to whatever no good they were planning,' the painter told Mackenzie.

When Mackenzie didn't answer, the painter laughed. 'You're a city girl, aren't you?' they asked.

'Yes. I'm staying in Colchester at the moment, which is quite small, but I'm from Sheffield, which is where I'm taking this today,' Mackenzie confirmed.

The painter laughed again. 'You really *are* a city girl if you think Colchester is *small*. The place is so big that just the thought of standing in amongst it all freaks me out,' they commented.

Being freaked out by thinking about standing in a busy place wasn't a concept Mackenzie understood. She wasn't sure what to say about it.

'If you're going to Sheffield today, then I'd best let you go. That's a long drive you've got ahead of you,' the painter said.

Mackenzie nodded. 'Thanks. I'd appreciate that,' she agreed.

When Mackenzie got back on the wide but twisty country lane, she thought: '*Even with the pretty river, I wouldn't want to live here. It's flat, it's quiet, and it has a terrible painter who is scared of big places but not crime.*'

A few moments later, Mackenzie thought: '*And Shaun doesn't live here, which is another thing against it.*'

'No Mackenzie, that's a good thing that he doesn't live here. He cheated on you, remember? He's not the nice guy you thought he was,' Mackenzie told herself out loud.

Even though Shaun, who wasn't the nice guy she'd once thought he was, lived there, Mackenzie was happy to be heading up to Sheffield.

13

Chapter Thirteen

The neighbourhood Mackenzie's parents lived in, like many neighbourhoods, had a hairdressers, a corner shop with a Post Office in it, a bakery, and two takeaways, all in a row. There were parking spaces in front of the businesses, one of which, after several attempts, Mackenzie put Jude's car in.

Having parked the car she'd borrowed, Mackenzie walked into the corner shop. When she saw the familiar white metal shelves crammed with items local people needed at all times of the day for high prices, she felt a rush of love for her surroundings, and a deep regret that they were no longer local to her. This confused her, because she hadn't felt any particular affection for the crammed corner shop when she'd lived five minutes away from it. The strong feelings she was experiencing unsettled Mackenzie. In an attempt to banish them, she took in a deep breath through her nose and slowly let it out through her mouth. It helped her a little bit, so she proceeded to the alcohol aisle.

The alcohol aisle of what had once been Mackenzie's local corner shop spanned the entire back wall. Mackenzie perused it in search of pink gin, tonic water, and bottles of bitter. The first, she located immediately.

Just as Mackenzie was reaching for what she thought was the nicest-looking bottle of pink gin, a voice behind her cried: 'Mackenzie Wight?!'

The shock of someone calling her name almost made Mackenzie make the expensive and messy mistake of dropping the bottle of pink gin in her hands. She automatically span round to see who had spoken, and saw a familiar face.

'Hazeem? You still work here?' Mackenzie asked the familiar face.

Hazeem let out a hearty chuckle. 'Of course. You've only been gone a few weeks,' he replied.

Until Hazeem pointed it out, Mackenzie had forgotten how short a period of time she'd been away from Sheffield for. To her, it felt like ten times as long, at least. The realisation she'd only been away for the length of some people's holidays rendered her speechless.

When it became clear Mackenzie wasn't going to answer him, Hazeem decided to ask her a question. 'Where'd you go? I know it was Down South, but I never found out any more than that,' he questioned.

Being asked a specific question helped Mackenzie regain the power of speech. 'Colchester, in Essex,' she told Hazeem.

'Oh, the Roman town with the oysters? I know the place,' Hazeem said.

It surprised Mackenzie that Hazeem, who had lived in Sheffield, South Yorkshire, his whole life, knew of Colchester, in Essex.

'What's it like down there?' Hazeem asked Mackenzie when she once again didn't answer him.

Three words popped into Mackenzie's head that described Colchester. 'It's not Sheffield,' she murmured.

'Right. I see,' Hazeem replied.

There then fell silence in the alcohol aisle. Much to Mackenzie's relief, it was broken by Hazeem's colleague calling for his assistance. This left her alone to collect her thoughts, and drinks for her family.

By the time Mackenzie was queuing for the till with a basket laden with alcohol, she felt more composed. The shop was busy, so there was a customer behind as well as in front of her.

'Eh, so *that's* what you spend it all on,' the customer behind Mackenzie muttered.

Not wanting to cause a scene, Mackenzie ignored the customer's comment. She didn't even turn round to see if she knew the person.

The customer at the till was filling out a lottery ticket. 'You never know. I might get lucky, like her down the road,' he remarked to Hazeem, who was serving him.

'If you do, I hope you spend it on more worthy causes than alcohol, such as our ruin of a church,' the customer behind Mackenzie said to themselves.

Though she didn't say anything out loud, in her head Mackenzie pointed out: '*It would be strange for me to invest in repairing the house of someone who I don't believe in.*'

When the lottery-ticket-buying customer finished buying his lottery ticket and left the shop, Mackenzie practically skipped up to the counter and placed her heavy basket on it.

While scanning Mackenzie's various bottles of alcohol, Hazeem remarked: 'Almost *everyone* who buys a ticket mentions you.'

For the third time in the space of ten minutes, Mackenzie couldn't think of what to say to Hazeem.

As she walked out of the corner shop with her now-purchased assortment of drinks, Mackenzie could feel the customer who'd been behind her glaring at her. She kept her head down and reminded herself that it didn't matter what people thought of her. She also reminded herself that people like that customer, as well as her ex-boyfriend Shaun, were why she'd been willing to leave Sheffield when her dad had asked her to keep an eye on her grandad.

The bags of alcohol Hazeem had handed her were heavy, so Mackenzie was relieved when she was able to put them down in the rear footwells of Jude's car. They couldn't go in the boot because that was where she'd put the painting that was the reason for her trip.

For the second time that day, a voice called out: 'Mackenzie Wight?!'

This time, Mackenzie span round to see the most familiar face of all. A face she had spent hours gazing at. The face of her ex-boyfriend, Shaun.

'Yes, I am. Being cheated on doesn't change your name, unless perhaps if you were unlucky enough to be married to the cheater,' Mackenzie replied.

Shaun was every bit as handsome as Mackenzie remembered. Her heart fluttered when she looked at him, but her flutters were nothing compared to the fiery heat of the anger that the sight of him inspired.

'And what about if you *weren't* cheated on? What about if you falsely accuse someone of something awful, dump them, and spread it about all over town, ruining their reputation? Does your name change then? You're qualified to know, Mackenzie,' Shaun retorted.

Judging by his flared nostrils and unrelenting glare, Shaun was every bit as angry as Mackenzie. That confused her, because *she* was the victim. *She* was the one who had a right to be angry. It also confused her that Shaun accused her of spreading news of his bad behaviour. She'd told her close family, but no-one else.

When they broke up, Mackenzie and Shaun spent hours arguing. She'd found it tiring, among other things. On a day when she'd driven hundreds of miles and been overwhelmed by nostalgia, she didn't feel like going through it again.

'I'm not doing this, Shaun. I've said everything I want to say, and you've had your chance to say your piece. It's done now,' Mackenzie told him.

'No, it's not! It's not done now! Not for me! I get the most vile looks from pretty much every female in the area, and it's all because of your lies! You've ruined me! All I did was love you, and you threw me in the dirt and painted yourself as some poor, poor, victim! Until you fix it, this isn't over!' Shaun yelled.

It made Mackenzie feel a little bit sick that not only had Shaun done a terrible thing, but he was denying it and accusing *her* of terrible things. He, the liar, was accusing *her* of lying.

'Even if your reputation is in tatters, and no woman ever goes near you again, it won't repair the damage you did to my heart,' Mackenzie replied.

Shaun folded his arms. '*Your* heart? The damage *I* did to *your* heart?! I did nothing! *You* tore *my* heart out and stamped on it so I can never give it to anyone again! I loved you like *crazy*! I thought you were the perfect woman. How do you think it felt when you turned on me for no reason at all? How do you think it felt, Mackenzie?!' he screamed.

It was clear to Mackenzie that Shaun was just going to go on and on at her, and she wasn't prepared to take that. Without another word to him, she jumped into Jude's car and slammed the door. Seconds later, she swung the car out of the parking space and shot off down the road, leaving behind a very angry Shaun and an equally angry driver, who'd had to emergency stop to avoid hitting her. The bottles of alcohol she'd stopped at the shop to buy clinked ominously in the footwells, but did not smash. They, and Mackenzie, made it to her family's house in one piece.

Chapter Fourteen

'I hate it, and you have the opposite taste in drinks to me, so I thought you'd like it,' Mackenzie told her sister, Britney, when she thanked her for buying tonic water and pink gin.

To show just how much she liked the drink Mackenzie had bought and mixed for her, Britney downed it in two gulps. She let out a happy sigh when she put the empty glass back on the kitchen side.

'Ta very much for that. You know me far too well,' Britney said.

As they'd known each other for almost twenty years, Mackenzie *did* know Britney well. She wouldn't say she knew her "far too well", because she thought it was a good thing to know a lot about her. Just because some of the things Mackenzie knew about Britney weren't good things, it didn't mean she thought it was a bad thing to know them. It meant that if ever their mum said Britney was out and not answering her phone, Mackenzie knew which friend to call to check if it was a hangover, a misplaced mobile, or something more serious.

To Mackenzie, her parents' kitchen felt far more relaxed than their lounge. That was because her mum and dad were in the lounge, but only Britney was in the kitchen with her. The sisters had excused themselves to wash up after dinner. Britney had brought her then-undrunk drink with her from the lounge, so she could sip it while waiting for Mackenzie to wash something so she could dry it. She hadn't expected to like it so much.

Washing up briefly made Mackenzie feel like she once again lived in the family home. Even when she'd been a busy student, she'd always found time to do the washing up. It was one of the first household tasks she'd been given, and one of the few she'd still been responsible for after becoming a uni student and girlfriend.

'Did you see Hazeem when you got the booze?' Britney asked Mackenzie, dragging her mind back to the present, in which she was a uni graduate who was single and had moved out of her hometown.

Being asked if she'd seen Hazeem reminded Mackenzie of who else she'd seen at the corner shop, or rather, *outside* the corner shop.

'I *did* see Hazeem,' Mackenzie murmured.

'Did he mention Shaun? I know they still play cricket together, so he might have done,' Britney questioned.

Only then did Mackenzie realise she was frowning, which her sister had probably noticed.

'I *saw* Shaun. He was going into the shop when I was going out,' Mackenzie told Britney.

A plate Britney was drying almost found itself on the floor. She regained her grip on it and her composure just in time.

'Oh my *goodness*! Did he speak to you?' Britney asked.

'Depends what you define as speaking. He *yelled* at me, but that's different,' Mackenzie replied.

'Oh, Mackenzie,' Britney murmured.

'He still doesn't admit he cheated, and is cross with me for accusing him of it. Worse than that though, he had a go at me for spreading news of it all over town. I've only told family, and I don't have that many relatives, so I don't know what he's going on about,' Mackenzie revealed.

Britney blushed and started paying close attention to the plate she'd been drying for over a minute. This sudden change in behaviour suggested to Mackenzie that she might know something about what Shaun had said.

'Britney?' Mackenzie asked.

'*You* didn't spread it all over town, but *I* did. I made sure every young woman in the area knew what he'd done, so he couldn't hurt them too,' Britney admitted.

Knowing Britney as well as she did, it didn't shock Mackenzie that she'd spread the word about what Shaun had done. It irritated her though, and she made that clear by crying: 'Britney!'

'What he did to you was vile, and the fact that he won't even admit it just makes it so much worse. I can't undo the hurt he caused you, or make him admit what he did, but I can cause him trouble by telling the world what he is. His name is mud around these parts now, and that's no less than what he deserves,' Britney replied.

Since speaking to Emma-Leigh, Mackenzie had wondered if she should forgive Shaun for what he'd done, even though he hadn't even admitted that he'd done it. The way Britney spoke about him left Mackenzie in no doubt that she was right not to. It also made her wish she didn't still have feelings for him.

15

Chapter Fifteen

Breakfast was Mackenzie's favourite meal of the day. It was the one at which there was the least conversation, and the most choice in what to eat. Her dad cooked a full English breakfast, only spoke to ask each diner which elements of the full English breakfast they wanted, and in what quantities.

'I was up all night watching this new show! I streamed the boxset, but I think it does actually broadcast on Sky Atlantic,' Mackenzie's mum told her and Britney, both of whom were sat with her at the dining table.

'Too early for this,' Britney mouthed at Mackenzie.

It wasn't necessary for Britney to explain what it was too early for. Mackenzie knew she meant it was too early for their mother to drag them into pointless chatter about American television. In order to avoid being dragged into pointless chatter about American television, Mackenzie simply didn't answer her mum.

Because of the presence of her mother, who insisted on talking early in the morning, Mackenzie decided that breakfast was one of the few things that was better in Essex.

Before Mackenzie's mum could speak again, Mackenzie's dad served up breakfast in its requested variations to his family. This ensured there would be no pointless chatter from anyone about anything for the next little while, because no-one can chatter away pointlessly when they have one of Mackenzie's dad's breakfasts in front of them.

As soon as her plate was empty, Mackenzie's mum spoke. 'How is your grandad, Mackenzie?' she asked.

A piece of sausage in her mouth prevented Mackenzie from answering her mother immediately.

'He's very well. I think he *is* lonely, but of course he'd never admit that,' Mackenzie eventually replied.

'And how about the business?' Mackenzie's mum enquired.

'The business? What about it?' Mackenzie questioned.

The only thing Mackenzie knew about her grandad's antiques business was that he went to the shop most days, and sometimes her uncle, Eddie, was also there. She wasn't interested in antiques, so had paid the business very little attention.

'Well, it's a delicate matter,' Mackenzie's mum told her.

Something told Mackenzie that whatever this "delicate matter" was, she was about to be dragged into it.

Knowing she was supposed to, Mackenzie asked: 'What is the delicate matter?'

'It's very difficult to say. Alf and I have not got any evidence of any wrongdoing *yet*,' Mackenzie's mum said.

'*How long is it going to take to find out what's wrong?*' Mackenzie wondered in her head.

Because Mackenzie didn't ask her what was up with the antiques business, her mum didn't tell her. Mackenzie just sat in silence, wondering what she was going to be asked to do.

'My brother, Eddie, has had a lot to do with the business since Mum and Dad split. He's also had a lot to do with Mum, who is still angry that she didn't get the business in the divorce. I'm worried that Eddie and Mum might be working together to damage Dad's business in some way, or steal from it,' Alf, Mackenzie's dad, explained.

As Eddie had moved to Essex when Mackenzie was little, she wasn't very close to him, and knew little about him. What little she *did* know was good, so it surprised her that he'd ruin or steal from her grandad's business.

'That's awful! Do you really think so?' Mackenzie questioned.

'We're not sure, and that's where you come in. We're hoping you'll take on a role in the business, and subtly keep an eye on what Eddie's up to while you're at it,' Mackenzie's mum said.

'As long as you're not doing anything. I wouldn't want to mess up any plans you had,' Alf hastily added.

Unbeknownst to her parents, Mackenzie *had* no plans *to* mess up. She hadn't yet worked out what to do in Colchester. Spying on her uncle wasn't an option she'd considered.

Looking for evidence that her uncle was up to no good wasn't something Mackenzie wanted to do, but she didn't want anything bad to happen to her grandad's business either. It seemed to her like the only decent thing to do was to get involved with the business.

'I'll see what I can do,' Mackenzie said.

'Thank you. It'd be a real weight off my mind if you'd look into this,' Alf replied.

'Well, looks like it's Detective Mackenzie to the rescue,' Britney commented with a smile on her face.

The word "Detective" made Mackenzie picture a magnifying glass. That lead her to think about glass in picture frames. It then occurred to her to wonder if the painting her mother had had her bring from St Lawrence was just an excuse to get her Up North again so she could ask for her help with the antiques business.

16

Chapter Sixteen

After tossing and turning for most of the night, Mackenzie managed to drift off just before sunrise. She intended to make up for her bad night by staying in bed for most of the morning, and she messaged her dad to tell him this.

That plan was ruined when the sound of Britney shouting woke Mackenzie at around nine o'clock. Concerned that Britney might be in trouble, Mackenzie pulled clothes on at great speed so she could get downstairs.

Outside the front door, Mackenzie found Shaun, who Britney was shouting at from inside the door.

'Leave us alone, Shaun! I don't want to see you, and we both know Mackenzie doesn't,' Britney yelled at Shaun as Mackenzie reached them.

When Shaun saw Mackenzie, he froze. He didn't speak or move. All he did was stare at her.

'He wants to talk to you. I told him you wouldn't want to see him, but he won't bugger off,' Britney told her sister.

'Why?' Mackenzie asked.

'I don't know. Because he doesn't understand that we hate him for being a pillock?' Britney suggested.

'No, I meant why does he want to talk to me,' Mackenzie explained.

The confusion between Mackenzie and Britney unfroze Shaun. He shifted his weight from foot to foot and broke his gaze from Mackenzie's.

'I need to apologise for my behaviour,' Shaun revealed.

If he apologises, can I forgive him? Can I rush back into his arms and be loved again? a part of Mackenzie's brain asked her. As if it was trying to support the case of that part of her brain, Mackenzie's heart beat so hard that she wondered if it would escape her chest. She wasn't sure how to answer herself, so she didn't.

'At last,' Mackenzie said in answer to Shaun.

'I don't want to just say sorry and then go away. Can you come out with me so I can explain myself?' Shaun asked.

The prospect of spending time with Shaun made Mackenzie's tummy gurgle. It seemed like an appropriate reaction to her, for the feeling was as *physically* unsettling as Shaun's presence was *mentally* unsettling.

Curiosity prevented Mackenzie from refusing Shaun. She simply had to know what he had to say. 'Yes, but I can't go out like this. Give me an hour or so,' she said.

'Seriously?' Britney mouthed at Mackenzie.

In response to Britney's silent question, Mackenzie nodded slightly.

'That's great, Mackenzie. That's really great. I'll meet you in town, I'll text you the location, and then I can properly apologise for being so horrid to you,' Shaun replied.

'Yes, you can,' Mackenzie agreed.

With nothing more to be said at that time, silence fell. During the silence, Britney looked at her in a way that made it quite clear she didn't approve of what she was doing.

'I'll be off then. Good to see you again, Brit, and I look forward to seeing you later, Mackenzie,' Shaun said.

As Shaun walked away, Britney yelled after him: 'It's *Britney* to you, and the pleasure was all yours!'

As there was no-one outside it anymore, Britney shut the front door. Without a word to her sister, she strode to the kitchen.

In need of a strong coffee, Mackenzie followed Britney.

'What are you doing? The man is scum, Mackenzie. Why have you agreed to be near him again? You moved hundreds of miles to get away from him, and now you're going out with him,' Britney questioned.

Like most kitchen's, Mackenzie and Britney's parent's kitchen had many hard surfaces, so Britney's words echoed. To Mackenzie, it felt like the room was amplifying her sister's anger. That feeling made her want to get out of the room and away from her sister as quickly as possible.

'I moved because Grandad was lonely. As for today, I agreed to see Shaun in town because I want to hear what he has to say,' Mackenzie replied.

'Grandad being lonely was a useful excuse. You needed to get away from Shaun, and no wonder. He hurt you, Mackenzie, badly. Please don't let him do it again,' Britney said.

In that moment, Mackenzie decided whether or not she'd get back together with Shaun if he apologised. She also decided whether or not to lie to reassure her sister. 'I won't let him hurt me, Brit. This will put an end to it all, and then I'll move on and find someone Down South,' she assured her sister.

Britney nodded. 'Good. I'm glad to hear it. I was worried for a moment there,' she told Mackenzie.

A thought occurred to Mackenzie. 'Thinking about people being worried, I don't think Mum and Dad should know about this. When they get back from the supermarket, can you say I'm just having a wander in town because I miss it? Can you not mention Shaun?' she asked.

'Of course. I won't say a thing to them about it,' Britney agreed.

Britney saying she wouldn't say a thing reminded Mackenzie that Shaun's number was blocked on her phone, so his text wouldn't get to her. As soon as she realised this, she whipped her phone out of her pocket and brought up her list of blocked numbers. She scrolled through numbers that had called to tell her she'd could claim compensation for an accident she'd never had, and others that had text to tell her she needed to click on a link to get a parcel redelivered, until she got to Shaun's. Her finger hovered over Shaun's number for a second before it tapped to unblock it.

Once they'd agreed not to tell their parents about the events of the morning, Britney made Mackenzie a coffee. A coffee that Mackenzie took up to her room so she could sip it while doing her makeup.

The familiarity of applying makeup soothed Mackenzie. Drawing a line around her lips absorbed all her attention.

Because Mackenzie was so absorbed by putting her makeup on, the interruption of her phone buzzing made her jump. She picked it up and discovered she had a text from Shaun. It read: "Forgot to say where in town we're meeting. I thought the park we used to eat chips in would be perfect, so I'll see you there."

For a moment, Mackenzie thought about leaving Shaun's number unblocked. She decided against that. Leaving his number unblocked would suggest she planned to use it again in future, and she didn't. After seeing him in the park, she never wanted to contact him, by phone or any other methods, ever again. Their meeting in the park was to be the official end of their relationship.

Chapter Seventeen

Standing on the tram on her way into Sheffield, Mackenzie wondered how Shaun was going to explain his behaviour. How *could* someone explain cheating? Even if he could *explain* it, he couldn't *justify* it. In her opinion, nothing could justify cheating.

Walking from the tram stop to the park reminded Mackenzie of just how much she'd missed Sheffield. She indulged thoughts about wishing the city was still her home because it stopped her thinking about Shaun.

'Thank you for coming,' Shaun said to Mackenzie when she reached him.

Mackenzie shrugged, as if agreeing to meet her cheating ex-boyfriend was no big deal.

'I guess I should get straight to it,' Shaun said.

'That would make sense,' Mackenzie replied.

Before getting "straight to it", Shaun started ambling down the path. Mackenzie followed him.

'I'm sorry for getting so angry with you. I thought only of myself. All I thought about was how horrid it felt to be accused of something I didn't do, and to lose a happy relationship because of it. I never considered the fact that, as you believe I cheated on you, you've felt all the feelings associated with that. You went through, and I guess *still are* going through, absolute misery, and I shouted and screamed at you as if it was your fault. It *isn't* your fault. It isn't *my* fault. It's the fault of whoever first made up lies about me,' Shaun told Mackenzie.

That was *not* the apology Mackenzie was looking for. Far from the long-overdue admission of guilt she'd been expecting, it was Shaun putting the blame on someone else's shoulders once more. If taken at face value, Shaun's words were nice, but Mackenzie didn't take them as face value. She assumed he was hoping to win her back.

When Mackenzie disagreed with someone, her arguments were usually cool and factual. She did often have strong feelings when someone couldn't see her point of view, but she kept them to herself. It was one of the biggest differences between her and Britney. Britney, when she came up against someone who didn't agree with her or something that wasn't quite how she wanted it to be, unleashed a tirade of emotions. If Britney wasn't happy about something, the whole world knew about it. Most of the time, Britney lost arguments, because although she made it clear she disagreed, she often failed to communicate *why*. Mackenzie usually resolved *her* disagreements in a satisfactory manner, because she explained her point of view well. In the case of her clash with Shaun though, she thought he wouldn't acknowledge her feelings if she remained calm. To make her feelings crystal clear, she adopted her younger sister's approach to arguing.

'Do you think I'll fall for that? Do you think I'll fall back into your arms and forget anything ever happened? Do you think you can keep seeing Kathy on the side and I won't notice?' Mackenzie asked with her hands on her hips.

'Kathy? As in Kathryn Carlisle, who works with you? Is that who I'm supposed to have cheated with?' Shaun questioned.

Until that moment, Mackenzie had never revealed who she'd been told was Shaun's bit on the side. She hadn't meant to reveal it then. It had just slipped out. That was something that wouldn't have happened if she'd used facts and logic to argue, instead of pure rage. As she couldn't take words back, there was nothing she could do about revealing something she hadn't intended to reveal. "What's done is done," as her grandad would say.

'You should know! You're the one who slept with her, even though you won't admit it!' Mackenzie snapped back.

'I can't admit to something that I haven't done! I almost wish I *had* cheated on you, just so I could apologise for it. I didn't though, so I can't. All I can do is apologise for how I treated you when you accused me of it. If it was *that* you hated me for, I'd understand. I was so careless and self-absorbed. How I've spoken to you since that horrible day is appalling. Nothing I say now can change that. I just hope I can show you I know what I did, and I feel terrible about it,' Shaun replied.

If Mackenzie had been acting like herself, she would've found it very hard not to believe Shaun and accept his apology. As it was, she was imitating Britney, who hated Shaun and thought he was the worst man on Earth, so it was easy to dismiss his words as yet more lies.

'Don't you try that again! I *know* you cheated. Trust me, the people who told me so wouldn't lie about such a thing,' Mackenzie retorted.

'They must have done. Whoever they are, they must have lied, because I know I didn't do anything,' Shaun argued.

'Like I say, they wouldn't. They're the last people in the world who'd ruin your happiness and reputation,' Mackenzie reiterated.

Shaun sighed. 'This is getting us nowhere, is it? We're just going round in circles, like we've done so many times before,' he pointed out.

That, Mackenzie couldn't disagree with. The discussion wasn't helping either of them, and was just like countless conversations that they'd already had. Unfortunately for her and Shaun, she couldn't think of a way forward. Nothing had changed, so their conversations couldn't change.

'I've said what I wanted to say, and I've taken up enough of your time now. I should go. I should let you go,' Shaun said.

Something about the way Shaun said he should let Mackenzie go sounded very final to her, as if he never expected to see her again. It also sounded very sensible, as arguing wasn't doing either of them any good.

'Yes. You've apologised for the thing you wanted to apologise for, and we have nothing new to say, so we should part now. That makes sense,' Mackenzie agreed.

'I wish you well in life, Mackenzie,' Shaun told her.

That confirmed Mackenzie's suspicions that he didn't think they'd meet again.

'I wish *I* could wish *you* well, Shaun,' Mackenzie said. It was the best thing she could think of to say. Once upon a time, she'd thought Shaun was wonderful, so she couldn't bare for the last words she said to him to be bitter ones, despite what she'd now been told about him.

Shaun nodded. 'I get it. You can't wish me well, because it would be odd to give good wishes to a guy who you think has cheated on you,' he replied.

'Exactly! If I've got everything all wrong, then I hope you have the happiest life imaginable. It's almost certain that I've been told right though, in which case I hope you have a miserable life,' Mackenzie explained.

A smile spread across Shaun's face. 'Thank you, Mackenzie. Because I know I've done nothing wrong, I can walk away knowing you want good things for me. That means a lot to me that I have your best wishes. Thank you,' he said.

As she watched Shaun walk away from her for the last time, Mackenzie shed a solitary tear. She told herself that that tear marked new beginnings in a new town with, eventually, a new man.

18

Chapter Eighteen

'So he *still* won't apologise?' Britney questioned after Mackenzie had told her about her conversation in the park.

As if he was confirming this for Mackenzie, the robin in the cherry tree by her and Britney tweeted.

'He can't apologise without admitting that he did it, and he'll never admit that he did it,' Mackenzie pointed out.

'But of course he did! His own parents wouldn't lie about such a thing!' Britney cried.

'He doesn't know that though. I haven't told him it was them that told me. I don't want him knowing they know what he gets up to, because then he'll hide it from them and any future victims. Apart from anything else, I can't bear to tell him that his own mum and dad sat me down in their lounge and told me their son was doing the dirty on me and I should have nothing to do with him. Can you imagine how it would feel to know your parents told your girlfriend that you're despicable and she shouldn't be with you?' Mackenzie replied.

The previously-tweeting robin darted from the cherry tree to Britney's feet, startling her.

'Pillock!' Britney declared.

'Shaun, or the robin?' Mackenzie questioned.

'Both, and it's nice to see a smile on your face,' Britney replied.

Until Britney had mentioned the smile on her face, Mackenzie had been unaware it was there. She too thought it was nice that she was smiling.

'Well, I get to spend another day here in sunny Sheffield with you, Dad, and also Mum, before going back Down South to find a man and something wrong with Grandad's business. I've got a lot to smile about,' Mackenzie pointed out.

From far above Mackenzie and Britney came a rumble of thunder.

Looking up to the sky, Britney said: 'I blame *you* for saying "sunny". Let's get in before the heavens open. Mum and Dad will be wondering what we've got up to anyway.'

Hand in hand, the two Wight sisters ran down the garden and leapt through the patio doors to the kitchen just before hail started pelting down.

Chapter Nineteen

'Your car is in the car park outside. Here's the key. Thanks again for lending it to me,' Mackenzie said to Jude when she met him in The Colneside Snooker Club a few hours after returning to Colchester. She put the aforementioned key in his outstretched hand.

'It's totally fine. It were great to spend quality time with Cecilia, so it's all worked out well,' Jude replied.

Before leaving Sheffield, Mackenzie had text Jude to ask when she should give him his car back. Jude had told her he'd be at The Colneside with Morton, and would appreciate it if she'd bring the car there (not in those exact words). She couldn't find a reason not to, so she had.

Something that Jude *hadn't* mentioned was that Emma-Leigh would also be there. Mackenzie was surprised when Emma-Leigh appeared from the main bar and walked straight up to the table next to Jude and Morton's.

'Hi! Cecilia told me you'd be here, so I thought I'd join you for a bit,' Emma-Leigh said to Mackenzie.

'Oh. I didn't expect that,' Mackenzie replied.

'I wanted to surprise you, so I did,' Emma-Leigh explained.

On her long drive from Sheffield to Colchester, Mackenzie had dreamt of running herself a hot bath after she'd dropped Jude's car off, and laying in it until it got cold. She was more than a little disappointed that that wasn't going to happen.

Not wanting to be rude, Mackenzie said: 'I'll set the balls up then.'

Playing snooker occupied Emma-Leigh until she left a good chance to make a significant break, which Mackenzie took. As soon as she found herself sitting in the uncomfortable chair provided for people who were unfortunate enough to be kept off the table by their opponent, Emma-Leigh was bored.

'Sheffield is a long way away. I wouldn't want to drive there,' Emma-Leigh commented.

'The drive to Sheffield was fine. It's major roads all the way. Before going there though, I had to go to a little village to pick something up for my mother. I hated those roads and got myself lost,' Mackenzie replied without taking her eyes off the snooker table.

'Was the little village on The Dengie? My Ronnie hates the roads out that way. He refuses to drive them, in fact, because there are loads of potholes that could ruin his car. They're just bend after bend, and lots of big vehicles seem to use them,' Emma-Leigh revealed.

The mention of big vehicles reminded Mackenzie of being stuck behind the boat on a trailer. She also thought about getting lost, and ending up in the village where the road ran into the river. As Emma-Leigh seemed to want to talk, Mackenzie decided to tell her all about it.

'The village I was looking for was called Saint Lawrence. I missed the turning and ended up driving as far as it was possible to drive, most of it behind a huge boat on the back of a lorry. The boat went off to a marina, I turned a corner, and the road literally went into the river. I've never seen anything like it!' Mackenzie told Emma-Leigh.

Emma-Leigh nodded. 'I know *exactly* where you ended up. I have a few friends who live there,' she replied.

Because Morton was about to play a shot as Emma-Leigh spoke, Mackenzie didn't answer immediately. She was mesmerised by how effortlessly Morton played a shot that left the white ball in the most awkward spot possible on the snooker table.

'I'm glad I accidentally ended up there. It was peaceful, there was a pretty view, and I had no signal, so no-one could bother me. It'd be a great place to go if you had a big decision to mull over,' Mackenzie eventually said.

'My friends like living there. As you say, it's peaceful. Apparently, the community is lovely too,' Emma-Leigh told Mackenzie.

As she found the game easy, Mackenzie chatted and played snooker at the same time. This meant that she didn't pay enough attention to where the cue ball went after one of her shots, so she left herself a thin cut to a blind pocket. That was challenging, even for her, so she didn't answer Emma-Leigh.

Only when Mackenzie fell silent did Emma-Leigh wonder if something had happened in Sheffield. It was, after all, the home of the ex-boyfriend who, from what Emma-Leigh could tell, had hurt Mackenzie badly.

'Is there anything in particular you'd think about while looking at the river?' Emma-Leigh asked, using what Mackenzie had said about the peaceful village as an opener for deep conversation.

'Nothing *worth* thinking about,' Mackenzie replied.

'Do you mean no-*one* worth thinking about?' Emma-Leigh questioned.

With Shaun's face in her mind, Mackenzie nodded. 'I saw him three times while I was away, but it's okay,' she told Emma-Leigh.

There was no need for Mackenzie to tell Emma-Leigh who she was referring to. Emma-Leigh knew exactly who she meant.

'Is there any chance of a reunion on the cards?' Emma-Leigh asked.

'No. Sorry to ruin the happy ever after in your head, but we're over. We did at least meet one last time to part peacefully. I even wished him well, provided that he's *not* the lying scumbag I've been told he is,' Mackenzie revealed.

'Right, so I'm free to find you a man down here,' Emma-Leigh replied.

It hadn't occurred to Mackenzie that talking about Shaun would prompt Emma-Leigh to renew her threat to "find a man".

On the table next to Mackenzie and Emma-Leigh's, Jude and Morton had just finished a frame. This meant the two men happened to hear Emma-Leigh's comment.

'*I'm* a man,' Morton pointed out.

When Morton spoke, Mackenzie stopped playing to listen to him.

'I think you've missed the point, Morton. I want to find a man for Mackenzie to date, not just *any* man,' Emma-Leigh pointed out.

'On the contrary, I've understood perfectly. I knew you meant that you want to find a man for Mackenzie to date,' Morton replied.

'No offence, Morton, but you're not the type of man I had in mind,' Emma-Leigh told him.

'I'm well-dressed and not what you would call ugly, so I believe it's reasonable to assume you wouldn't suggest Mackenzie dates me because I have an unusual personality. If that is the case, then I'd like to point out that you only know I have an unusual personality because you know me. If you did *not* know me, then you might suggest me as a potential date. It is perfectly possible that someone else well-dressed and not ugly also has a personality that's incompatible with Mackenzie's. Therefore, it will not be possible for you to find a man for Mackenzie, for you can't tell by looking if they're suitable,' Morton said.

For a few seconds, Mackenzie, Jude, and Emma-Leigh all stood and stared at Morton. Two of them were amazed by the great logical argument Morton had made, and one of them was irritated that she didn't know how to respond.

To distract herself from the fact that she couldn't answer Morton, Emma-Leigh got her phone out to check Facebook. At the top of her News Feed was a photo Ronnie had posted twenty minutes ago of himself holding a half-full bottle of red wine under the words: "This won't be lasting long. Thanks for the recommendation Lauren". When she saw the photo, Emma-Leigh sighed loudly.

'What's up, Emma-Leigh?' Jude asked.

To answer Jude, Emma-Leigh showed him the picture of Ronnie with the wine. 'He's supposed to be picking me up later. Obviously, he's forgotten about me,' Emma-Leigh explained.

'Yeah, looks like it. I can take you back after this frame, now that I've got my car back,' Jude offered.

When she noticed Mackenzie wasn't playing snooker anymore, Emma-Leigh showed her Ronnie's post.

When she saw it, Mackenzie thought: *'Interesting that Emma-Leigh isn't bothered that another woman recommended wine to him. Considering his history, that would bother me. I must be paranoid.'*

'Can you believe it?' Emma-Leigh asked Mackenzie.

Based on what she'd been told about Ronnie, Mackenzie *could* believe it. What she couldn't believe was that Emma-Leigh put up with him.

Having told her friends about the latest thing her boyfriend had done, Emma-Leigh put her phone away.

'Do I get to play yet?' Emma-Leigh asked Mackenzie.

'No. I only stopped because I was listening to Morton. I'm still at the table,' Mackenzie replied.

'So I still have to sit here and do nothing?' Emma-Leigh questioned.

'Yes. That's how snooker works,' Mackenzie confirmed.

With the knowledge that she'd be in it for some time, Emma-Leigh flopped back in her chair.

It worked out that Morton and Mackenzie both cleared their tables at the same time.

'Looks like we've both lost. If it's okay with Mackenzie, I'll get you home,' Jude said to Emma-Leigh.

Just as she was about to say it was fine with her for Emma-Leigh to go home, Mackenzie realised *she* couldn't get home. She'd driven Jude's car from her grandad's house to The Colneside, but as she'd now returned it to Jude, she couldn't drive it back. She could get a taxi back, but she'd had several taxi rides since she'd moved to Colchester and didn't want to pay out for another one.

'I might need you to give me a lift, if you don't mind. I used your car to get myself here and didn't think about the fact that I wouldn't have it to get myself home,' Mackenzie said.

Jude chuckled. 'That's the sort of mistake *I'd* make. Don't worry about it. I'll take you home too,' he replied.

Under a lamppost in the car park behind The Colneside, with its front right tyre on the right line of its parking space, was Jude's Suzuki Swift. A few spaces along from Jude's car, equidistant between and parallel to the lines of the space it was in and also under a lamppost, was a Toyota Yaris. The Toyota's hazard warning lights flashed when Morton pointed his key at it.

'My car is less impressive than my friend Jude's, but it serves its purpose,' Morton said.

'I don't really like my car. A friend were selling it when I were looking for a car, so I ended up with it. There's nothing wrong with your car, Morton,' Jude replied.

As Mackenzie took one last look at the lump of concrete she'd played snooker in, she wondered when she'd next get to play snooker.

'Do you often come here by yourself, Morton?' Mackenzie asked.

'No. That time you saw me was a one-off. I only usually come when Jude's here. The game provides useful entertainment and negates the need for conversation, so it suits us,' Morton replied.

'Are you busy on other nights?' Mackenzie asked.

The thought of being busy of a night-time made Morton snort. 'No. I don't have anyone to be busy with,' he told Mackenzie.

An idea was forming in Mackenzie's head. She had a feeling that looking for trouble at her grandad's business was going to be stressful, so she wanted to know she had a way to unwind.

'I wondered if you'd like to play snooker with *me* one night,' Mackenzie said.

Morton stared at Mackenzie in wonder. 'Did you just volunteer to spend time with me?' he questioned.

'Yes,' Mackenzie confirmed.

'Why?' Morton asked.

It confused Mackenzie that Morton was so surprised she'd asked to play snooker with him. She couldn't fathom why Morton would think people didn't want to spend time with him.

It was hard for Mackenzie to explain why she wanted to spend time with Morton, so she just said: 'I like you, Morton, and you give me a good game of snooker.'

This stunned Morton so much that he couldn't speak.

Before jumping into the back of Jude's car, Mackenzie told Morton: 'I'll get your number from Jude and call you to arrange to meet up.'

As Jude drove her home, Mackenzie thought about how pleased she was to not have to drive having already driven hundreds of miles that day. She also thought about how pleased she was to have arranged to meet up with Morton. She'd left Colchester with no idea what to do there and only one friend, who she didn't have much in common with. She'd returned with a secret mission and the potential for a friendship with someone who she considered to be more like herself.

20

Chapter Twenty

In the absence of anything better to do on the Monday morning that followed her return to Colchester, Mackenzie watched old episodes of *Grand Designs* on her iPad. An episode about a keeper's lodge by a London cemetery intrigued her. It wasn't just the techniques used in the restoration of the gothic Victorian building that fascinated her. The man who owned the building came from a very wealthy family, and yet his project ran into various difficulties and he got very stressed about them. It was the first time she'd seen someone with millions of pounds struggle. She found it comforting, and sympathised with the man.

When that episode ended, Mackenzie decided that she should probably get up. She'd showered, brushed her hair, and brushed her teeth hours ago, but had then returned to bed. All she had to do was find a clean pair of jeans and a t-shirt in her drawers, pull them on, throw a cardigan over that, and walk down the stairs.

On Monday mornings, Mr Wight could usually be found sitting in his armchair, watching the various fly-on-the-wall documentaries shown on BBC One at that time. This meant that Mackenzie was surprised when she discovered that the lounge was empty.

Voices coming from outside inspired Mackenzie to look through the window. In the garden beyond it stood her grandad and a woman who looked like she was around his age who she didn't recognise, talking about a plant.

To find out who the woman was, and what she was doing in her grandad's garden, Mackenzie stormed outside.

When he saw his granddaughter, Mr Wight cried: 'Ah, here's my Mackenzie! She's the clever one I was telling you about.'

'And who is this? What's she doing in your garden?' Mackenzie asked, nodding at the woman she didn't know.

'I'm Hazel. I live next door, you see, so I couldn't help noticing what a state your garden is in. Ron used to tell me that I shouldn't stick my nose in where it's not wanted, but I can't bare to see poor plants suffer like this,' the woman said.

'Well, with all due respect to your Ron, he is plain wrong. Your little nose *is* wanted here. The flowers, and bushes, and whatnot that I have in here did nothing to deserve me. I don't *mean* to treat them so badly, but, as you've discovered, I'm clueless. Your help will be really welcome,' Mr Wight replied.

Under the sun, Mackenzie found that her cardigan was unnecessary. She shrugged it off and tied the arms around her waist. In the time it took her to do that, neither Mr Wight nor Hazel explained what plans they'd made in her absence.

'What are you going to do then?' Mackenzie asked.

'She's going to help with the garden! Isn't that nice?' Mr Wight revealed, gesturing at his garden, which was anything *but* nice.

'Mow the lawn every week or so, plant out some summer bedding, deal with weeds, check that your spring-flowering bulbs are all far away enough from each other, that sort of thing,' Hazel explained.

If Hazel had spoken in Greek, it would have made as much sense to Mackenzie. When she'd left school, she had promised herself that she wouldn't study anything that didn't interest her. Horticulture had never interested her in the past, still didn't interest her, and she believed it *never would* interest her.

Despite not being interested in horticulture, Mackenzie could see that the garden she was standing in needed attention. You didn't need an expert eye to spot the weeds thriving among the long grass, and notice the absence of flowers and healthy shrubs. The poor state of the garden was as clear to see as the many years that had passed Mr Wight by.

'So, this is your granddaughter. Is there anyone else living in that sweet little cottage with you?' Hazel asked.

Mackenzie folded her arms. 'What's it to you?' she questioned.

A frown added to the wrinkles on Mr Wight's face. 'Be nice, Mackenzie! It's just me and her in there, and I'm sorry for the rudeness shown to you by someone living under my roof,' he said.

With a dismissive swipe of her hand, Hazel replied: 'Oh, don't worry, George! I appreciate a blunt woman, or a blunt *anyone*, come to think of it. All this pussyfooting around these days gets on my nerves. Say it how it is, that's what I think. Don't dress it up or avoid the difficult subjects. As you asked so nicely, I'll tell you that the reason I'm asking is because I'm lonely and was thinking of inviting you two over for a cuppa one day, but, if there had been more of you, I might not have. My kitchen is a bit cosy. It's not from an era where entertaining your friends and showing off to them was the biggest priority. In that way, it's a bit like me.'

As they were both naturally blunt, Mackenzie and Mr Wight grinned. They saw each others smiles, and knew they were both thinking: *'We've found a kindred spirit.'*

The shock of finding someone who thought like them Down South rendered Mr Wight and Mackenzie speechless.

'Oh, maybe that came across wrong. I do understand that you have to handle delicate matters with care sometimes, and that there's all this pressure to perform and that's why some people go all out to impress. I didn't mean to sound judgy. I hope I haven't offended you. You seem so lovely. I don't want to offend you,' Hazel rambled.

'Eh? Why would you think we're offended?' Mr Wight questioned.

When it dawned on Mackenzie why Hazel thought she and her grandad were offended, she explained: 'We *loved* what you said. *That's* why we fell silent. We're just stunned that someone else thinks like us.'

'So, you liked it?' Hazel questioned.

'Yes!' Mr Wight and Mackenzie cried in unison.

Now *Hazel* was speechless. The only sound around her was the buzzing of the various insects who liked the many weeds in the garden. She wasn't listening to them though, or anything in real life. Her mind was replaying words it had heard in the past.

Mackenzie's voice brought Hazel back to her senses by asking: 'Hazel, are you with us?'

'Oh, yes, of course! Sorry, I drifted off for a moment there,' Hazel replied.

'Wherever you drifted to didn't look very pleasant,' Mr Wight commented.

Hazel licked her lips and fixed her gaze on a daffodil that was more brown than yellow. Paying close attention to the black plastic toggles, which were smooth to touch, she wrapped her red duffle coat around her and did it up.

'I've got a bit of a chill. I must go. Goodbye, George and Mackenzie. I'll be back, as long as you don't mind that,' Hazel told the grass.

As Hazel dashed out of his garden, Mr Wight called after her: 'Thanks for popping over. Nice to meet you!'

Once Hazel was out of earshot, Mr Wight looked at Mackenzie expectantly. When she didn't say what he expected her to say, he asked: 'So, what did you think?'

'I'm not sure,' Mackenzie murmured.

'I liked her. Thought she was a good sort, and it's lovely of her to help out with all this,' Mr Wight said, gesturing at his garden.

Even before Mr Wight had said so, Mackenzie had known that he liked Hazel. What she *didn't* know was why Hazel had *really* left.

21

Chapter Twenty-one

The list of contacts on Mackenzie's phone was full of memories. Seeing one name, Kathryn Carlisle, caused her to recall events she'd rather forget. She swiftly scrolled past it, and dozens of other names, to get to the bottom of her list. There, she found contact details for Edward Wight, the person she wanted to call.

'Yeah, this is Eddie. Who wants me?' Edward Wight asked when he accepted Mackenzie's call.

Never before had someone answered the phone to Mackenzie like her uncle just had. It amused her so much that she roared with laughter.

'Mackenzie? Is that you?' Eddie asked.

Surprise cut Mackenzie's laugh off abruptly. 'You know me by my laugh!' she cried.

'Yeah! Of course I do! No-one I know, or have ever known, laughs like that. It's not changed since I moved down here all those years ago,' Eddie confirmed.

No-one Mackenzie knew, or had ever known, had recognised her just by her laugh. No-one except her uncle Eddie just then.

'So, what do you want?' Eddie asked.

'A job in Wight's Antiques. I've not long moved, but I'm already bored. I fancy helping out at the family firm, and Grandad told me to call you. He said that admin would be best for me, because I've got a head for numbers, so he says, and that's your department,' Mackenzie explained.

'Moved? Down here you mean? In Essex? But Sheffield suited you so well! Whyever would you move?' Eddie questioned.

'Yes, Essex. I've moved in with Grandad in Colchester. He was lonely, so I thought I'd come down and keep him company,' Mackenzie replied.

In Colchester, Mackenzie was gazing out of her bedroom window, which looked down on the garden. A garden which her grandad and Hazel from next door were in.

In a village near Colchester, Eddie was trying to remember if all the paperwork for Wight's Antiques was in order and correct. Paperwork which it was his job to ensure was accurate, that Mackenzie would see if she started helping with the admin.

'But you're an architect! Admin isn't the same as architecture. Besides, it's not like you need the money,' Eddie pointed out.

'I'm so bored that I'd stack shelves in ASDA for free if they'd let me. This isn't about money. It's about having something meaningful to fill my time. At the architectural practice that employed me in Sheffield, I hardly ever got to do any actual building design. I was really the tea girl, and I answered the phone when there was no-one else to. Admin will be fine. My teachers at school always said I was a fast learner, so it won't take me long to get the hang of it,' Mackenzie explained.

Looking anything *but* bored was Mr Wight, down in his garden.

Mackenzie watched him shake, presumably with laughter, as Hazel pranced around the garden with her head held high.

'If Dad, your grandad, agrees, then I guess I can find something for you. We can't have a bright lass like you getting bored. Having said that, I'm spending all day today looking for burlwood tables. I'm not sure if you can call that entertaining,' Eddie agreed.

Having grown up with relatives who worked in the trade, Mackenzie thought she knew a lot about antiques. The fact that she'd never heard of a burlwood table made her question that.

Part of Mackenzie didn't want to admit to a man who she wanted to employ her that she had no idea what he was talking about. The other part of her really wanted to know what a burlwood table was. Curiosity won, so she asked: 'What is a burlwood table?'

'Burlwood is wood with burls in. A burl is a tree growth with funny grain. Burlwood is all the rage at the moment, because it's rare and looks different. It's used a lot for coffee tables,' Eddie revealed.

'Ah, I see. Thanks for that,' Mackenzie said.

'Not a problem,' Eddie replied.

On Eddie's end of the line, there was a decisive click, followed by the drumming of fingers on wood.

'Have you found something?' Mackenzie asked.

'Looks like it. I need to call the dealer and ask a few questions, so I'll have to hang up on you now. I'll have a think about what you can do and get back to you,' Eddie said.

'Great, thanks for that! I look forward to hearing from you,' Mackenzie enthused.

'Yep, no problem. Bye now,' Eddie replied just before ending the call.

When she put her phone on the windowsill, Mackenzie noticed two things. The first was how warm it was in her room. The second was that Hazel and Mr Wight were no longer laughing. They were both leaning on spades, clearly deep in conversation. Something that was said prompted Hazel to remove a hand from her spade and place it on Mr Wight's shoulder. That was when Mackenzie snatched her phone back off the windowsill and flopped down onto her bed.

As she lay on top of her quilt, staring up at the ceiling, Mackenzie wondered what Hazel wanted from Mr Wight, and if she ought to interfere in some way.

22

Chapter Twenty-two

The long, thin case in her left hand earned Mackenzie quite a few curious looks, not that she noticed. She was too busy dreaming about using the item in the case to pay any attention to the people staring at her.

Getting the case on the bus was challenging. Mackenzie sat by the aisle and leant it against the seat next to her. As the bus swept around the roundabouts on the way into Colchester, she absent-mindedly steadied the long case with a hand.

When Mackenzie reached her destination, she started paying more attention to her case and the many expensive and breakable arcade machines around it.

After taking care not to hit her case on the arcade machines, Mackenzie ensured she didn't bash it on the ceiling or floor as she went upstairs to the snooker club.

'Fun to carry one of them, isn't it?' the man behind the bar called to Mackenzie when she reached the top of the stairs with her unbashed case.

'Yes, but it's worth it,' Mackenzie replied.

The man behind the bar looked at Mackenzie in a way that suggested he'd expected her to say more than that. When she thought about what his job was, she understood why.

'I'm here to play against a friend, Morton. He should already be here with a table set up,' Mackenzie explained to the man whose job it was to take people's money in exchange for use of the snooker tables his employer owned.

'Ah yes, I know Morton. He came in half an hour ago with a tall ginger bird. Not his girlfriend, apparently. They both laughed when I suggested they were a couple,' the man behind the bar told Mackenzie.

'Thanks,' Mackenzie replied.

As she made her way through the unoccupied pool tables to the snooker room, Mackenzie wondered who the "ginger bird" was. When she'd text Morton to arrange a time to meet up for a rematch, he hadn't mentioned anyone else tagging along.

At one end of the snooker room, Morton was attempting to pot the black. He was being watched by a woman who fitted the description that the man behind the bar had given.

'So, is this Mackenzie?' the ginger woman asked just as Morton took his shot.

The way Morton struck the cue ball made a sound that even someone who didn't play cue sports could tell was wrong. As Mackenzie *did* play cue sports, she knew the noise was a miscue. It had probably happened because Morton had been distracted.

'*Mackenzie*? You came?' Morton questioned.

'Yes. We did arrange to meet up today,' Mackenzie replied.

'I told you she'd come,' the ginger woman said.

Morton opened his mouth, but no words came out.

'I'm Tamsyn, a friend of Morton's. I have a free evening that I don't want to spend at home with my housemate's Westie, and

Morton didn't want to wait for you by himself all night and then go home alone when you didn't show. Apparently, no-one would actually voluntarily spend time with him. I think that Jude, myself, and now you, disprove this,' the ginger girl revealed.

When she realised Morton thought she didn't want to see him, and had thought she wouldn't turn up, Mackenzie was, like him, speechless.

'Because I knew Mackenzie would show, I've got the latest Nadiya Hussain book in my car to take to Cecilia's. See you another time, Morton. Thanks for completely thrashing me. Nice to meet you, Mackenzie,' Tamsyn said when neither of the people she was with spoke.

'Yes, you too, Tamsyn,' Mackenzie murmured.

Both Morton and Mackenzie watched Tamsyn walk out.

At the opposite end of the long room full of snooker tables, a young man was lining all the red balls up down the middle of his table. He was the only other person in the room, and, as he'd not finished setting the table up to his liking, he wasn't playing. This meant that Mackenzie didn't feel guilty about having an in-depth conversation with Morton.

'Why were you so sure that I wouldn't come? I said I would. In fact, I said I wanted to, and was looking forward to it,' Mackenzie questioned.

'Because I really am terrible company. I'm dull. Clever, but dull. Why would a bold and fun girl like you want to hang around with me? As you said, you did agree to, but surely you did that because you felt pressured to. You needn't have worried though. I'd never pressure anyone to spend more than a few minutes in my company. I'm not a sadist,' Morton replied.

Being called "bold and fun" put a smile on Mackenzie's face. The rest of what Morton said made her want to cry. The only time she'd thought herself as unlikeable as Morton believed himself to be was the first couple of months after splitting with Shaun. At all other times, she'd had no self-confidence issues. The first month or two that followed Shaun's parents' shocking revelation had been so dark, Mackenzie tried not to think about them. Somehow, she'd got through them. As remembering how she'd coped might help Morton, she allowed her mind to drift back to that time.

When she looked back on it, Mackenzie found that many things had contributed, and were contributing, to her recovery from the place she'd found herself in the wake of her break-up. One thing in particular stood out to her. The realisation that it hadn't been about her, but Shaun. Nothing she'd done justified Shaun cheating, and it didn't say anything about her.

'*Are* you dull, or do other people make you *feel* dull? Is it really about you, or them? Just because some people call you boring and laugh at the idea of hanging out with you, it doesn't mean you're not entertaining and worth hanging out with. What others think of you often has no correlation to who you actually are,' Mackenzie questioned.

'Well, I'm not well placed to answer that. I don't find myself dull, but of course I don't. I like being a stickler for detail, and focused, and intellectual, and having niche interests. Being awkward, often not knowing what I ought to say to people, and having a stammer, I like less, but I've learnt to live with all that. You are right the things people think about me aren't always true. Maybe I'm *not* dull? Maybe it *is* Maybelline? As someone who doesn't use make-up and can't judge myself objectively, I can't say. Thanks for questioning it though,' Morton replied.

'It's nothing, Morton. All I can say about you is that I enjoy spending time with you. I think Jude and Tamsyn do too,' Mackenzie said.

'Jude has been such a good friend to me for so many years, and it's nice to have Tamsyn to hang out with every now and again. As for you, I don't know how to express the joy I felt just now when you said you enjoy being with me,' Morton revealed.

In the dark, quiet, room, Mackenzie could feel how much her words meant to Morton. Their eyes happened to lock briefly, and in that moment she felt as if they were the only two people in the world. Morton was all that was on her mind, and her only aim for the next little while was to show him how much he mattered to her. She related to him so strongly, and therefore she connected with him. In the back of her mind, part of her was wondering if they were meant to meet up. If her break-up with Shaun, and other things that had followed that, had all happened so she could be standing there on that day with Morton.

The sound of a leather tip striking a Phenolic resin ball brought Mackenzie round from her trancelike state. It reminded her that, like the man practicing on the table at the opposite end of the room, she was there to play snooker.

'Let's get these balls set up so we can play. I'll take on the baulk colours and the blue if you'll do pink, black, and the reds,' Mackenzie said.

'Yes, of course,' Morton agreed, already moving around the table to retrieve the balls Mackenzie had mentioned from the rails by each pocket.

Once the balls were set up, Mackenzie removed her cue from its case and screwed the two parts together. Just touching the cool ash of her cue made her smile. The stick of wood had so many memories ingrained in it.

As he'd already played snooker that evening, Morton's cue was out of its case and ready to use. This meant he could watch Mackenzie assemble hers and admire it. 'Good cue. Personally, I prefer a one-piece, but I'd have any John Parris. At least, I would have any John Parris, if I could afford it,' Morton commented.

It hadn't occurred to Mackenzie that someone would know how expensive her cue was. She could tell Morton was wondering if she was rich. Her financial situation wasn't something she wanted him, or anyone, to think about.

'Yes, I got it at a car boot. Seller didn't know what he'd got, bless him. I practically stole the thing for what it cost me,' Mackenzie lied.

After taking a breath, Mackenzie said: 'It's amazing what you can get at car boots. I didn't used to go to them much, because I objected to getting up early on a Sunday, which was always when they were on, when I got up every day for work. I should've thought to go to one round here in the last few weeks, as I've been unemployed. I'll be working again come Monday though, so it's too late now.'

'Wow, you were lucky to find something as sublime as that cue at a car boot,' Morton replied.

While walking to the bottom of the table, Morton asked: 'Am I breaking?'

As the man at the opposite end of the room was down on his shot, facing away from her, Mackenzie nodded.

Eyes blazing with concentration and competitive spirit, Morton lowered his upper body and his cue over the snooker table. In a manner that suggested he had all the time in the world, rather than the three hours and eleven minutes until the light over the table turned off, he guided his cue back and forth. It teased the shiny white cue ball, but never quite made contact. Then, after a pause, Morton allowed his cue to gently tap the cue ball, sending it on its way off the triangle of reds and back down the table. A few seconds later, it came to rest not far from where it had started.

'Oh, silly boy,' Morton muttered to himself.

As the snooker room was a quiet place, Mackenzie heard Morton reproach himself under his breath. When she looked at the snooker table, she couldn't see any reason for him to be unhappy.

Gesturing at the snooker table, Mackenzie pointed out: 'Your shot was perfect. You're not a silly boy.'

'Oh, you heard me? Sorry. That wasn't about the shot. It was about the fact that I didn't think to ask you what your new job is, or if you're looking forward to it. *That's* silly. I know you're supposed to pick up on these things and ask thoughtful questions, but I completely missed it,' Morton explained.

Mackenzie laughed, which prompted the man at the opposite end of the room to pause his practice and stare at her briefly. 'Don't worry about it! If I wanted to talk about my new job, which is admin for the family antiques firm, then I'd have made it quite clear. I don't play games, except snooker. I'm a straight-talking woman,' she replied.

'As opposed to a gay, mute, man?' Morton questioned.

At first, Mackenzie wondered if she'd misheard Morton. As there was very little background noise, that seemed unlikely, but his words made no sense to her. 'What are you going on about?' she asked.

'It was a joke. You said you were a straight, talking, woman. The opposite of that, approximately, would be a gay, mute, man. It was meant to be funny but, as usual with me, it was just strange,' Morton explained.

'*Oh*, now I get it, sort of,' Mackenzie said.

For a few seconds, Morton reflected on the conversation so far. Based on his recollection of it, he suggested: 'Shall we play snooker now, as talking isn't going very well?'

'Talking is going fine, but yes, let's play,' Mackenzie agreed.

When she took another look at where Morton had left the white ball, Mackenzie regretted agreeing to end the conversation to play. It looked like snooker wasn't going to go very well.

Chapter Twenty-three

When Mackenzie got out of the van at Battlesbridge, her eye was drawn upwards by the industrial giant before her. It was obvious to her it was a place that had been built for a purpose it was no longer needed for. She worked this out mostly by looking at the architecture. The building's name, The Old Granary, also helped Mackenzie reach her conclusion.

'And this is the antiques centre. Hopefully we'll find some bargains in here,' Eddie said, gesturing at the tall and thin building Mackenzie was staring at.

'Uh-huh,' Mackenzie murmured.

As she walked with her uncle and grandad to the entrance, Mackenzie gazed up at the imposing structure she was about to enter.

As the building was so large, Mackenzie had imagined it would feel spacious inside. It did not. Every inch of the antiques centre seemed to be crammed full of people and objects. The place was teeming with life. It reminded her of a city centre. There was lots to see, and lots of other people seeing it.

'First, the most important step in antiques hunting,' Mr Wight said as he guided Mackenzie and Eddie through the building.

After entering a stairwell, Mackenzie asked: 'What's that?'

Mr Wight didn't answer. The only noise in the stairwell was that of their footsteps. Footsteps that went on relentlessly for almost a minute as Mr Wight led his party all the way to the top.

'Have tea and a bite to eat. For the dealers' sakes, never browse and negotiate on an empty stomach,' Mr Wight replied as he strode into the room at the very top of the building.

When Mackenzie followed her grandad, she found herself in a tearoom. Bunting hung off the beams, and mismatched wooden chairs at PVC-adorned tables lined the narrow space. Something about the tearoom made her feel lighter.

After pausing by a table, Mr Wight said to Eddie: 'Let Mackenzie sit by the window, as she's never been here before.'

As directed, Mackenzie sat in the seat by the window. Out of that window, she saw the road, and a river running away as far as she could see beyond that. Being able to see so far took Mackenzie's breath away.

'I think she likes it,' Eddie commented.

'It's stunning! I love that this place is so tall. I can see for miles,' Mackenzie replied.

Mr Wight leant over to Eddie and fake whispered: 'And she hasn't even tried the cake here yet.'

—

So that Mackenzie could try the cake made and sold by the proprietors of the tearoom, Mr Wight ordered some of the chocolate variety from a smiling lady in an apron.

With the important business of ordering cake out of the way, Mr Wight sat back and gazed out of the window. The view was nothing compared to what he'd seen in and around his hometown, but it still absorbed him and allowed his mind to wander peacefully.

Across the table from Mr Wight, Mackenzie was occupied by the same view and, similar thoughts to, her grandad.

After a few seconds of silence, Eddie began fidgeting. 'So, erm, Mackenzie... What have you been up to recently?' he asked.

Mackenzie sighed inside as her uncle's voice dragged her mind back from the aimless wandering she'd been enjoying. 'I played snooker with a nice lad,' she told Eddie.

As soon as he realised he'd started what would be a lengthy exchange, Eddie felt more comfortable in his chair. *'Great! Snooker is my niece's greatest passion. Even if she doesn't want to talk about this boy she played with, she can go on about the game she played with him until the cake comes. No more dead air, thank goodness,'* he thought.

'What's the boy's name? What was he like?' Eddie asked.

'Morton. He's no confidence, bless him, but I like him. Yes, I can see that he's not everyone's cup of tea, and he's got a lot of rubbish in the past from people because he's not normal, but, as *I'm* not exactly normal, I think he's great. He's kind, clever, polite, and plays a mean game of snooker. So good that he beat me, though only the once,' Mackenzie replied.

'He beat you? He's not that polite then. You're a girl. A girl he doesn't know. Wouldn't it have been polite to let you win?' Eddie questioned.

Mackenzie scoffed. 'No! What's my being a girl have to do with anything? It's not polite to let me win. It would have been offensive! Doing his very best to beat me, thus treating me as his equal, which I am, was the politest thing he could have done,' she argued.

The passion with which Mackenzie spoke left Eddie with no response. Once again, silence fell.

'The sunlight looks nice on the river,' Mr Wight pointed out.

This inspired Mackenzie and Eddie to gaze out of the window.

Much sooner than Mackenzie had expected, the same happy-looking lady who'd asked Mr Wight what he wanted returned with the cake he'd requested. It was in the form of three wedges on patterned china plates.

'Are you trying to fatten me up?' Mr Wight asked, pointing at the triangle of cake on the plate that had been delicately placed in front of him.

'Well, you're one of our best customers, George. It's only fair to give you decent portions,' the lady who'd brought the cake over replied.

While smiling to herself, the lady who'd brought cake walked away.

While smiling at the cake a lady had brought him, Mr Wight said: 'Right, there shall be no more talking. Time enough for that when there's not cake to be enjoyed.'

Once cake had been enjoyed, Mr Wight lead his son and granddaughter around the antiques centre below the tearoom. As she knew very little about antiques, Mackenzie's role was just to observe and write down details about the items Mr Wight bought in a notebook she'd been given.

As they were walking through an aisle, Eddie stopped abruptly. 'Ooh, I want that,' he said, pointing at something.

It took Mackenzie a moment to realise the rectangular lump of metal with three dents in it and red paint flaking off that Eddie had pointed to was a petrol can. The only thing she could see that made it at all interesting was the three dents looked like the eyes and mouth of a face. It was as if the petrol can was smiling at her.

Mr Wight did not smile at the petrol can, or his son. 'Are you sure?' he questioned.

'Yes, very sure. It's perfect,' Eddie replied.

'That's not the word I'd have used to describe it, but if you really want to get it then I'll find the dealer,' Mr Wight said.

Whilst her grandad went off to talk to the owner of the petrol can, Mackenzie stared intently at her notebook. Having just seen how much influence he had over her grandad, she didn't want to talk to Eddie.

24

Chapter Twenty-four

Since moving to Colchester with his then-wife, Mr Wight had had a shop just down the road from the bus station. Two decades after first signing the lease, Wight's Antiques were still at that shop. It was there, in the office at the back, that Mackenzie got acquainted with the paperwork.

'Eddie deals with this lot these days. Really, he should explain it to you. He's at his mother's today. I'm sure he will take you through it all tomorrow. You're welcome to have a look through it all though. A clever lass like you can probably work it all out,' Mr Wight told Mackenzie when she asked to get started on the admin.

Unbeknownst to Mr Wight, it wasn't necessary to tell Mackenzie Eddie was at his mother's. Her mother had somehow already found out and told her. It was the very reason she'd chosen that day to take a look at the office.

It took Mackenzie a few minutes to work out that, in addition to official documents, and journal rolls from the till that kept a record of every transaction that had gone through the till on the day they'd been printed, there were notebooks. A quick flick through told Mackenzie these notebooks contained records of items the business had purchased, what stock the business had and where it was stored, as well as records of what had been sold. Having worked out what they were, she put the notebooks back in the drawer they'd come from, and made a mental note to check them one day to make sure everything was accounted for.

The office was dominated by a Victorian partners desk made of ash. Once upon a time, it had sat in the directors office of a railway company. Now that it was in the office of an antiques shop, each drawer was labelled. Mackenzie opened the one marked: "Payroll". She wanted to know how much Eddie earned. Documents inside the drawer showed that her grandad's salary was the Real Living Wage.

The Real Living Wage was an amount Mackenzie recognised thanks to discussions with her previous employer. They'd paid her the National Living Wage, which was the legal minimum for someone of her age. She'd argued that they ought to at least give her the Real Living Wage, an amount deemed by an independent organisation to be what someone needs to get by in life. The employer refused. At the time, she'd been in a mood to fight and change things rather than give up and find another job. None of the discussions she'd had with her bosses had improved her job, but it pleased her to know she'd tried.

Knowing her grandad paid himself enough to live on, but no more, made Mackenzie's heart swell with pride. The absence of Eddie's name on the payroll paperwork made her head ache with confusion.

As there was nothing more she could learn from the payroll paperwork, Mackenzie returned it to the drawer. It was odd that Eddie wasn't on the paperwork, but she couldn't see anything sinister about it.

Just as Mackenzie was closing the payroll drawer, Mr Wight

walked into the office. 'Ah yes, we'll need to pay you. Eddie can sort that tomorrow. It'll be the Living Wage, if that's okay with you. The proper one, not the one that the government somehow think you can live on,' he said.

'Oh, you don't have to pay me! Grandad, it's not like I need the money. I just want something to occupy my time,' Mackenzie protested.

Shaking his head, Mr Wight took the seat opposite Mackenzie at the desk. It was a chair usually used by visitors, and was a lot softer than he realised. After unexpectedly sinking into his chair, Mr Wight told Mackenzie: 'Yes, you're working because you *want* to, and that's great. I one hundred percent appreciate that you don't want to sit around all day. However, you are working just as hard as Eddie and I, so you deserve to be paid.'

'But that's ridiculous! Why should a little family business pay a multimillionaire who's only working for them because she's bored?' Mackenzie questioned.

Mr Wight tutted. 'It's not about your bank balance. It's about you working for a business. This isn't about you. It's about Wight's Antiques, an employer that doesn't need volunteers,' he replied.

When Mackenzie drew breath to argue once more, her grandad gave her a look that silenced her. At that point, she knew she'd lost.

'Don't bother arguing. I won't give in. Where do you think you got your independence and stubbornness from?' Mr Wight said.

Mackenzie laughed. 'Good point. You are to blame for me being this way. Alright then, I'll let you pay me,' she conceded.

'Good. Now, I'm just going to pop out for some milk. There's a lady looking at the mirrors at the moment. Could you stand at the counter and watch her? If she decides to actually buy something, just keep her talking until I get back. I won't be long,' Mr Wight told Mackenzie.

As it was her job, and she couldn't think of any reason why

she wouldn't want to, Mackenzie agreed to keep an eye on the shop floor.

The lady looking at mirrors got a phone call a minute after Mackenzie started watching her and left the shop to take it. No other customers entered, so she had the shop floor to herself.

On top of the one-hundred-year-old little pine and mahogany counter that Mackenzie was standing behind was a notebook and pen. Without really thinking about it, she flicked to an unused page and put pen to paper.

It was only when Mr Wight returned with two litres of milk that Mackenzie acknowledged what her hands had been up to.

'Is that a proper plan for that dream house you used to draw with crayons when you were little?' Mr Wight asked Mackenzie.

The fact that her grandad remembered the waxy multi-coloured drawings she used to slave over for hours made Mackenzie smile. Not only did he remember them, but he remembered them in detail. Either that or he was good at guessing.

'It *is* a floorplan for a version of it, yes. The woman by the mirrors left, and I automatically started sketching,' Mackenzie explained.

Mr Wight nodded. 'Good. I'm glad you're still using your talents,' he replied.

It had been a long time since someone had told Mackenzie she was talented. The last person to say so had gone on to break her heart. Though she didn't think her grandad was going to break her heart, she didn't know how to accept his compliment.

When he realised he wasn't going to get an answer from Mackenzie, Mr Wight told her: 'I'm going to make tea now. I'll take yours to the office when it's done, so you can get back to whatever it was you were doing.'

Once she was back in the office, Mackenzie got out the notebooks that listed all the items the business had in stock. In an attempt to get Shaun out of her head, she scoured them to ensure everything was accounted for. Some items, she recognised, as they'd been purchased on the trip to Battlesbridge that Eddie and Mr Wight took her on. Others were completely unfamiliar to her, but that didn't matter. What mattered was that there were some items that were noted in the book of purchased stock, but not the inventory, or the record of sold items. It was as if they'd vanished.

Chapter Twenty-five

Mr Wight insisted that Mackenzie had to have two days off. The reason he gave was that Eddie did, and he did, so it was only fair that she did too.

As the first of those days off coincided with her mum's day off, Mackenzie called her family home.

'Dawn Wight speaking. I'm free to talk. At least, I'm free until four. I'm going out to see Misty O'Brien then. I was just looking through the post. All useless sales rubbish, of course. Nothing I actually wanted. These people who send junk mail waste so much of our time. Honestly, it's ridiculous! We have lives to get on with! Lives that aren't improved by adverts about water softeners and conservatories,' Dawn Wight, Mackenzie's mum, told the person she'd just answered the phone to.

It was clear to Mackenzie that, if she didn't speak at that very moment, she wouldn't get to. 'Yes, I know who you are. This is *Mackenzie* Wight,' Mackenzie Wight replied.

'Ah, Mackenzie! I'm glad *one* of my daughters has the decency to call me!' Mackenzie's mother cried when she answered the house phone.

The sound of the front door opening distracted Mackenzie. As far as she knew, she was the only one home, and Mr Wight wouldn't be back for hours. Unsure of what to do, Mackenzie stayed put.

Whoever had just entered was wheeling something on casters into the lounge. There then came a thud as the someone rolled the thing on casters into the wall.

'Really, Henry?! How dare you behave like that?! Now be a good boy and let me work. I've got to get back for Ronnie,' the newcomer to the house cried.

It was then that Mackenzie realised the person downstairs was Emma-Leigh, and she'd crashed her vacuum cleaner. For the first time in several seconds, she allowed herself to breathe.

'Have you seen this new show on Netflix? The one with that man from the thing that everyone raved about when you were little? Oh, it's brilliant! It's amazing! I was watching it last night with your dad, and oh my word, the ending! Mackenzie, you would not believe what happens!' Dawn cried.

'No. Grandad doesn't have Netflix, and neither of us watch much telly. I called to talk about my job. The one you asked me to get. I may have discovered something,' Mackenzie told her mum.

Below her, Mackenzie heard the whirr of a vacuum cleaner. For the first time, she wondered why Mr Wight was paying Emma-Leigh to clean when his granddaughter was living with him and bored.

'Discovered something? Now, that's interesting. You're like Sherlock, although you're nowhere near as handsome as Benedict Cumberbatch. That's good though. I do have a bit of a thing for him, and it would be very weird if I fancied my own daughter,' Dawn said.

At that moment, Mackenzie was glad her mum couldn't see her, for she cringed. She didn't want to know who her mum fancied.

'The business has comprehensive records of its stock, how much it cost us to buy, where it is, and if it has been sold. I *say* comprehensive, but there are irregularities. There are some items which are on the list of items Wight's Antiques have purchased, but they aren't on the other lists. They're not on the inventory, but they haven't been sold,' Mackenzie revealed.

'Ah, so he stole them! He stole them and gave them to his mother to spite your dear grandad,' Dawn cried.

'Hang on a minute, Mum! Not necessarily! There's nothing yet to say uncle Eddie stole anything, or that my grandmother is involved. It's just an oddity, that's all. Another strange thing I discovered is that Eddie isn't on the payroll paperwork,' Mackenzie replied.

'He could be up to no good though! You know how furious your grandmother was that she couldn't get her mitts on the business. She'd do anything to get back at George. Eddie is a bit of a weakling and easily lead. It was the first thing I noticed about him. Your dad cooked his shepherd's pie and invited me and Eddie over to the flat he was living in at the time. This was back when Eddie still lived in Sheffield, but George and your grandmother were already down in Essex. It was a tiny place, that flat, but it was all he could afford. Anyway, we were all crammed into this flat, eating shepherd's pie and chatting about this and that, and Eddie just agreed with everything I said. No opinions of his own. He just sat there, nodding his head. So, what I'm saying is, if your bitter grandmother wants to get back at George, it'd be easy to manipulate Eddie,' Dawn said.

Internally, Mackenzie sighed. As yet, she wasn't convinced that her uncle had done anything wrong. Her mum jumping to conclusions wasn't going to help anyone, and she didn't want to be a part of it. As far as she was concerned, the conversation was finished. Her job was done. She'd passed the information on, and there was no need to hear what her mum made of it.

'Right, I need to go now. I'll let you know if I discover anything else interesting. Say hi to Dad and Britney for me, and take care of yourself. Goodbye now, Mum,' Mackenzie said.

'Oh, you're going? Well, I guess I'll go back to doing little bits around the house. I have to make the most of my day off to catch up on things,' Dawn replied.

'Yes, that's adulthood for you. Bye now,' Mackenzie agreed, hanging up as soon as she'd finished speaking.

A few minutes after finishing one conversation, Mackenzie decided to go downstairs and have another one. One she might actually enjoy.

Mackenzie found Emma-Leigh in the kitchen, wiping down the worktop.

'I didn't know you were here when I arrived. Am I bothering you?' Emma-Leigh asked.

'No. I just thought I'd say hello. I haven't seen you for a little while,' Mackenzie replied.

Like many people, Emma-Leigh would rather chat than clean. Unlike many people, cleaning was her job, so she spent a few seconds running her cloth over the only bit of worktop she hadn't yet touched before she allowed herself to fully engage in conversation with Mackenzie. That way, when Mackenzie left her to continue working, it would be easier for Emma-Leigh to remember what she'd already done.

'I've had lots of work on, and that and being with Ronnie has just taken all my time. I haven't even managed to find you a man yet. Don't worry though. I won't give up,' Emma-Leigh told Mackenzie.

When Mackenzie realised Emma-Leigh hadn't forgotten about finding her a man, her heart sank. The heart that was still broken into a thousand pieces. As she desperately tried to work out how to convey to Emma-Leigh that she wasn't ready to date, all Mackenzie could feel was the beating of her actual heart, which evidently was intact.

'One of my friends will have a handsome and single brother. Maybe one of my old classmates will reconnect with me through social media. One of the hot ones, whose Facebook relationship status is "single". Don't worry. I'll find someone,' Emma-Leigh assured Mackenzie.

The thought of Emma-Leigh finding someone made Mackenzie perspire, despite the spring breeze wafting in through the windows. She wished something to put a stop to Emma-Leigh's matchmaking ambitions would fly in.

A bit like a breeze through a window, an idea of how to deal with Emma-Leigh drifted into Mackenzie's head. There was something she could say that would definitely prevent Emma-Leigh matchmaking. Before she went ahead and said it, Mackenzie considered if there was any way the lie she was about to tell could cause trouble in the future. She came to the conclusion that it couldn't. Going on a date with Emma-Leigh's sister's friend, or whoever it was she'd end up finding, would cause more than trouble. There was no way she could allow it to happen.

'Don't you dare try to match me up with a random acquaintance of yours. I've got my eye on someone, and I don't want you messing things up,' Mackenzie said.

The biggest grin Mackenzie had ever seen appeared on Emma-Leigh's face. 'Really? I'm so happy for you! Who is the lucky man who has caught your attention? Anyone I know?' Emma-Leigh asked.

Mackenzie licked her dry lips. 'Yes. It's Morton,' she replied.

26

Chapter Twenty-six

When she walked through her grandad's garden, Mackenzie noticed all the changes Hazel had made. The mowed and weed-free lawn, the bold poppies springing up between the paving slabs, and the new wooden trellis archway all caught her attention. It looked like her grandad had poured a lot of money into his garden, based on Hazel's advice. Mackenzie wondered if her expert gardener next-door neighbour had shares in the local garden centre. It would explain Hazel's sudden interest in Mr Wight.

On the fence to the left of Mackenzie sat a pigeon. When she looked up to her right, she saw another pigeon and a crow, also sitting on a fence. Above the fence, she could see the top of a bird feeder, which the crow flew to when the sparrow who had been there flitted off to another garden. One of the pigeons on Mackenzie's right flapped across the garden to sit on the other fence. It was then that she realised the birds were queueing for the feeder. 'How British,' she thought.

All the queueing birds darted off in alarm when Mackenzie's

phone rang. When she took it out of her pocket and saw her sister's name on screen, she assumed their mum had told her that Eddie was a thief, and Britney was calling to see if this was actually true.

After sliding her finger across the screen to answer, Mackenzie said: 'No matter what Mum has told you, uncle Eddie isn't a master criminal in league with our estranged grandmother. There's just something odd about the paperwork, that's all.'

'This isn't Britney,' a familiar male voice replied.

'Shaun!' Mackenzie cried.

The few birds in Hazel's garden that hadn't been alarmed by Mackenzie's ringtone were startled by the volume of her voice when she recognised her ex-boyfriend on the phone.

'Yes. Britney is here, I've not nicked her mobile. That's what I'm calling you about,' Shaun told Mackenzie.

Finding out that Britney and Shaun were together startled Mackenzie as much as her voice had startled the birds around her. Britney hated Shaun even more than Mackenzie herself did. Why would she be with him?

'What?' Mackenzie questioned, unable to articulate.

'It's a long story. Are you sitting down?' Shaun asked.

'The one thing Hazel didn't make Grandad buy is a bench,' Mackenzie thought as she looked around herself.

As Shaun had asked if she was seated, Mackenzie decided that she probably should be. 'Hang on. I'm out in the garden. Let me get back indoors,' Mackenzie told Shaun.

While running across the garden, Mackenzie heard the slapping of her trainers on the paving slabs, and vomiting on the phone. She knew it was Britney throwing up. She'd held her hair back after one too many enough times to recognise the sound.

'Don't worry. Britney is okay,' Shaun reassured her.

As she slammed the back door shut, Mackenzie wondered if Britney really *was* okay. From the little information Mackenzie had gathered so far, her sister was at Shaun's, she was ill, and he had her phone. None of that seemed okay to Mackenzie.

Eventually, Mackenzie reached the lounge. She perched on the sofa and said: 'Tell me what's going on, and why the hell my little sister is with you.'

'I was in a bar last night. So was Britney. She was all alone, absolutely bladdered, and couldn't pay her tab. A member of staff was rowing with her about it, and threatened to call the police on her. It was ridiculous. I couldn't just leave her there, so I...' Shaun started to explain. He was cut off by footsteps.

'Why have you got my phone, and who are you talking to? Please tell me you haven't called my mum,' Mackenzie heard Britney say.

'No, I wouldn't call your mum. This is your sister. I wanted to let her know where you were and ask what to do with you, but I know she's blocked me. You were sleeping, so I didn't think you'd mind me taking your phone,' Shaun told Britney.

Just as Mackenzie was going to ask if she could speak to Britney, Britney asked: 'Can I speak to her myself now I'm up?'

When Mackenzie heard Shaun hand Britney her phone, she found it easier to breathe. If he was letting her talk, everything must be okay.

'He paid for my drinks, Mackenzie, and then he rescued me. Not just a few drinks either. I practically drank the place dry. Frankie abandoned me after we had a bit of a disagreement, but Shaun, the guy whose name I dragged through the mud on your behalf, saved me. I'm so ill, Mackenzie! I mean, I would be, that's what happens when you drink pretty much everything on the drinks menu, but *girl* do I feel rough! This is the hangover to end all hangovers, which is why I'm crashing at Shaun's. Usually, I'd stay with the friend I'd got drunk with while I slept it off, but of course she abandoned me. I could just about handle the car journey across town, but listening to Mum waffle on about American telly when I get there would be too much,' Britney ranted.

A picture was beginning to come together in Mackenzie's head. Britney had gone out for drinks with Frankie, a friend she'd known since primary school. They had a row about something, and Frankie had stormed out, leaving Britney angry and with access to as much alcohol as she wanted. Shaun, for his own reasons that weren't relevant, went to the same bar as Britney. By the time Shaun gets there, it is impossible not to notice what a state Britney is in. When he recognises Britney, Shaun takes her home to keep her safe, paying her tab for her so that the bar let her leave. It was mostly clear to Mackenzie what had happened and why. The biggest missing piece of the jigsaw was Shaun's motive for helping Britney. As far as Mackenzie knew, Shaun hated her and her sister, yet he'd gone above and beyond to help. There had to be a reason.

When she started thinking about how to advise Britney, Mackenzie recalled two things from her conversation with their mum. One of them, she would mention to her sister. The other was that their mum had said: "I'm glad *one* of my daughters has the decency to call me." Mackenzie had thought nothing of it at the time. Now, she wondered how long Britney would have to be away from home and out of contact for before her mum did more than just moan about it.

'Mum is going out to see Misty at four. You could get home then and go straight to bed. Dad won't be back from work yet at that time, so you'll have no-one to answer to. In the meantime, see if you can eat porridge with banana on top. It's always worked for you in the past,' Mackenzie suggested.

'Oh, you're a genius, Mackenzie! Yes, that's what I'll do. Porridge with banana sounds so appealing, and it's great that I can avoid Mum. I'm sure Shaun won't mind popping to the shops to get the necessary bits, and running me home after four. He's already blown off lunch with a mate for me, so his whole day is free,' Britney agreed.

Helping her sister made Mackenzie feel more like herself than she had in months.

After giving orders to Shaun, which Mackenzie overheard, Britney said goodbye to her big sister and handed the phone over.

'I owe you an apology,' Shaun told Mackenzie as soon as he had Britney's phone back.

Is this it? Is this when he admits the affair? Do I finally get to forgive him? Mackenzie wondered.

In the background on Shaun's end of the line, Mackenzie heard Britney walking out of the room. She guessed she was going to the bathroom.

'What are you apologising for?' Mackenzie questioned.

'When I ran into you outside Hazeem's place recently, I said to you… Well, *screamed* at you, that you'd ruined my reputation. You didn't though. I know that now. You kept it quiet and private. It was your sister who spread the lies about me far and wide. I should have guessed that. You always have been measured and thoughtful. Bad-mouthing someone isn't your style. It very much *is* Britney's style though. I know how angry she can get, and I know that you mean the world to her. What she did, she did out of love and loyalty, and I can hardly blame her for that,' Shaun explained.

A part of Mackenzie was gutted that it wasn't the admission and apology she'd hoped for. Another part was pleased Shaun now knew it was Britney who'd dragged his name through the mud. She was touched that he could see the love between her and her sister, and that he understood why Britney had done what she'd done.

As Shaun had done so much for her beloved little sister, it was hard for Mackenzie to keep at the front of her mind that she was furious with him for cheating and not even admitting it. If Shaun hadn't helped Britney, goodness knows what would have happened to her.

'Thanks for rescuing Britney, and for looking after her so well. We've been horrible to you at times, and yet you saved her. I really can't express how much it means to me. Of course, I will reimburse you for the bar tab you settled, but I ought to do more. I don't know what I can do though,' Mackenzie said.

Shaun sighed. 'It was just the right thing to do. What happened between us wasn't relevant. I couldn't leave her there knowing something bad could happen to her. Cheers for saying you'll pay me back for her tab. I'd be happy for you not to, but I don't want to hurt your pride, so I'll let you,' he conceded.

It gave Mackenzie flutters that Shaun knew it would offend and hurt her if he refused to let her pay him for settling Britney's tab. It was a small reminder of how he had once known her inside out.

Trying to ignore her flutters, Mackenzie asked: 'Would you like me to let you get on with making Britney porridge with banana?'

'Yeah, I guess so. I do need to nip down to the shops to get a banana. Britney seems much more well now, so that's okay. When I drop Britney at home, I'll tell her to let you know she's back safe,' Shaun agreed.

'Good. Thanks again for everything. Goodbye now,' Mackenzie said.

'Farewell, Mackenzie. I'm glad Britney needed my help, because I've loved talking to you. Bye for now,' Shaun replied.

When Shaun ended the call, Mackenzie's finger itched to call him back. With all her self-control, she managed to fight the impulse. That same self-control didn't allow her to ignore the feelings she had for Shaun, but it helped her manage them.

27

Chapter Twenty-seven

On one of those days when you can comfortably leave home without a jacket, but you don't work up a sweat strolling along the street, Cecilia took Emma-Leigh to the Tea Rose Cafe for lunch. As Emma-Leigh discovered, it had a courtyard, which made it the perfect place to eat on a day like that.

Without giving it much consideration, Cecilia delicately placed herself in a lightweight metal chair at one of the not-so-light metal tables.

With as much thought as Cecilia, but less poise, Emma-Leigh flopped into a chair. The chair tilted backwards for a second, but Emma-Leigh got her heels on the ground and shifted her weight forward before the chair rocked past its tipping point.

'Ah, this is nice! I love being outdoors,' Cecilia said.

Emma-Leigh's phone buzzed. Before it had stopped vibrating, she had her mobile in her hand.

'Who is it?' Cecilia asked, folding her arms.

As she was still reading the message she'd just received, Emma-Leigh didn't answer.

While she waited for Emma-Leigh to turn her attention back to the real world, Cecilia read the laminated menu that had been left on the table.

Only when she'd read the message, answered it, and returned her phone to her pocket did Emma-Leigh tell Cecilia: 'It wasn't Ronnie, so as it turns out I could have ignored it. It was Mackenzie, the girl who lives with Mr Wight, the kind, Northern man with the pretty cottage who I clean for.'

It occurred to Cecilia that, if Jude text her, she'd want to read his message immediately. She wouldn't if she was talking to someone in the real world, but she'd want to, and if she heard she'd got a text, until she read it she would wonder if it was Jude. This thought prompted her to uncross her arms.

'I hear a lot about Mackenzie from Jude. She's making friends with Morton, and Jude says he keeps mentioning her. Apparently, Morton can't understand why a "clever, funny, and not-ugly young woman like Mackenzie" wants to hang out with him,' Cecilia commented, using her fingers to make air quotes to show that she was describing Mackenzie as Morton had.

Emma-Leigh rubbed her hands together and grinned. 'Oh, this is great!' she cried.

'Yes, it is. Poor Morton doesn't really have any friends, except Jude, and he's a good man really,' Cecilia agreed.

It wasn't just Cecilia and Emma-Leigh who were taking advantage of the sunshine to enjoy The Tea Rose Cafe's courtyard. Two other tables were occupied, both by couples. One of the couples were gasping as milkshakes were placed in front of them.

The woman who had placed milkshakes on one table made her way over to Cecilia and Emma-Leigh. 'Afternoon, ladies! What can I get for you?' she asked.

'Oh, I've not read it yet! Give me a minute,' Emma-Leigh replied.

'I'd like egg and chips, please, and orange and lemonade,' Cecilia told the waitress.

It pleased Cecilia to see the waitress jot down her order on a notepad.

When she looked up from the notepad, the waitress noticed two things. The first was that Emma-Leigh was still looking at the menu. The second was that both she and Cecilia were in direct sunlight. Behind the waitress was an umbrella. Its shadow didn't quite reach the table, or the people sat at it.

'Would you like me to move this for you?' the waitress asked, gesturing at the umbrella that could protect Cecilia and Emma-Leigh from the sun.

'That's most kind. Yes, please,' Cecilia agreed.

After the waitress moved the umbrella so that its shade covered her, Cecilia realised how hot she'd been, and how pleasant it was to be in the shade.

'Panini, that's what I'll have! A bacon, brie, and cranberry panini... With tea,' Emma-Leigh declared.

The waitress's pen flew over her notepad. 'Great! That sounds lovely. I'll get that off to the kitchen, and I'll be out with your drinks in a minute,' she said.

On her way back inside, the waitress paused at one of the occupied tables to pick up completely empty plates. While there, she asked the customers who'd emptied their plates if they'd enjoyed the food.

The waitress's hard work didn't go unnoticed by Cecilia, who marvelled at her efficiency.

'Ah, yes! I was about to tell you something interesting regarding our friends, Mackenzie and Morton,' Emma-Leigh said.

Cecilia didn't speak. She knew Emma-Leigh would take this as an invitation to chat about their friends.

Just as Cecilia had predicted, Emma-Leigh revealed: 'Mackenzie is single. Her ex cheated on her, apparently. When I found out, I told her I'd make it my mission to find her someone. She wasn't best pleased about this. I thought it was just because she doesn't think she's ready for love again yet. As it turns out, that's *not* why she doesn't want me to find her someone. Mackenzie doesn't want me to find her someone because she's already found herself someone. That someone is Morton! She's got her eye on him!'

'Well, that would explain why they've been spending so much time together,' Cecilia replied.

For a few seconds Emma-Leigh stared at Cecilia. When she realised she wasn't going to get the shocked reaction she'd been hoping for, Emma-Leigh said: 'It amazes me that *anyone* fancies Morton, let alone Mackenzie! He's so quiet, and she's bold and fiery. I guess he's not *ugly*, and she's not exactly a stunner, not in your league for sure, but even so, it really shocked me when Mackenzie told me she'd got her eye on him. Maybe they'd be a good match though, as they're both snooker geeks.'

Once upon a time, if someone had told Cecilia that another woman was not in her league, she'd have assumed that other woman was in a league far above her. At that moment in time, Cecilia knew Emma-Leigh meant that she was far more beautiful than Mackenzie. It didn't matter though, because nowadays she thought it was irrelevant what she, or any other person, looked like. She took it as a sign of Jude's influence. There were certain moments when he complimented particular aspects of her appearance, but most of the time he didn't comment on her looks, just like she didn't often comment on his.

'Good luck to Mackenzie and Morton. I know from personal experience that you can meet the love of your life at a snooker club,' Cecilia commented.

'It won't just be down to luck. I'll play my part. I'm taking them both to the zoo this weekend, because neither of them have been before. If I see an opportunity to nudge them together, it'd be rude of me not to take it,' Emma-Leigh replied.

Cecilia tutted. 'Please, you are Emma-*Leigh Layton*, not Emma *Woodhouse*. Just because you successfully helped one couple get together, it doesn't mean you should play matchmaker with another,' she told Emma-Leigh.

'Who is Emma Woodhouse?' Emma-Leigh asked.

The big rectangular planters and stark black lantern in the centre of the otherwise-featureless courtyard caught Cecilia's attention as she wondered whether or not to explain to Emma-Leigh who Emma Woodhouse was.

When she spotted the waitress approaching with drinks, Cecilia was very grateful.

'Thanks... I'm sorry, I don't know your name,' Cecilia said to the waitress as she placed her orange and lemonade in front of her.

'Oh, I'm Shirley, and you're welcome. It's my job,' the waitress, Shirley, replied.

'A job you do most well,' Cecilia told Shirley.

Shirley grinned. 'Thanks. I haven't been here long. Nice to know I'm doing alright,' she said.

The courtyard was overlooked by the cafe that used it, a couple of empty retail units, and some flats. From that cafe, someone yelled Shirley's name.

Upon hearing her name, Shirley left Cecilia and disappeared into the cafe.

When Cecilia sipped her orange and lemonade, she was satisfied with her choice. The light bubbles tickled her tongue as it refreshed her. The drink did everything a non-alcoholic drink should do.

After Emma-Leigh picked up her tea, and she placed her glass back on the table, Cecilia tried to recall what they'd been talking about before being interrupted. Upon remembering, she decided to take the opportunity to move the conversation on.

'Do you know any good jewellers? They don't have to be in Colchester. I'm happy to drive if you know one that stocks a variety of styles or is reasonably priced,' Cecilia asked.

Emma-Leigh considered this, but didn't think about the fact that her friend was changing the subject. 'There are several in town, but I don't know if they're good. I think I remember there being a decent one in Chelmsford. I'd have to ask one of my sisters to be sure. Jewellery isn't really my thing,' she replied.

'Thank you. There's no rush,' Cecilia told Emma-Leigh.

While trying to work out which of her sisters would be most helpful, it occurred to Emma-Leigh that, like her, Cecilia didn't often wear jewellery.

When she worked out why Cecilia wanted to know about jewellers, Emma-Leigh gasped. 'Do you want a ring for Jude? Are you going to propose?' she asked.

'Maybe,' Cecilia answered, smiling at her drink.

28

Chapter Twenty-eight

When Emma-Leigh pulled up outside Mr Wight's in her Renault Clio Expression, Morton was in the front.

As soon as Mackenzie came out of her grandad's house and approached the car, Morton got out of it and pulled the front passenger seat forward.

'You're shorter, so I thought you'd go in the back,' Morton said to Mackenzie.

Emma-Leigh gasped. 'Morton! Be a gentleman and let Mackenzie sit in the front!' she demanded.

The shade of red that Morton's cheeks turned almost matched the car he was standing next to. When he felt able to look up from the floor, his gaze met Mackenzie's. 'Sorry. In my mind... I thought it was com... I was being sensible. I didn't mean to be rude,' he stammered and mumbled.

Shaking her head, Mackenzie clambered into the back of the car. After putting her seat belt on, Mackenzie told Morton: 'It wasn't rude. Look, I fit perfectly fine back here. You can have the front.'

While Morton put the front passenger seat back in the right position and sat on it, Emma-Leigh commented: 'That's love, getting into the back of a small car for someone.'

Neither Mackenzie nor Morton said anything to that.

Once Morton had his seat belt on, Emma-Leigh turned the key to start the car. The car responded by choking for a second or two before settling on a steady hum.

'Right, off to the zoo we go!' Emma-Leigh declared.

As Emma-Leigh forced her way through the streets of Colchester, Mackenzie gazed out of the window. Every street they turned onto had different architecture. Much of the housing she saw was utilitarian and lacked any individuality. It took her a while to realise this was because it was military and ex-military housing.

The variety of the buildings that had always been intended for civilians pleased Mackenzie. Sitting in the back of Emma-Leigh's car, she almost fell in love with Colchester.

One of the things that prevented Mackenzie falling in love with Colchester was the temperature. Just six minutes into the journey, she was sweating.

'If I pay you a fiver for fuel, will you let me put the air-conditioning on?' Morton asked.

'*Oh, I love you, Morton!*' Mackenzie thought to herself.

After slowing down to allow an oncoming van to duck out of her way on a road narrowed by parked cars, Emma-Leigh replied: 'No, because I don't have air-con.'

It took Morton a second to absorb the fact that there was a car built in in the 21st century without air-conditioning. Accepting that such a vehicle existed was even harder for him when he thought about who owned it. He saw Emma-Leigh as a show-off, but her car didn't fit with that image. It made him question his opinion of her. Something didn't add up.

'Why do *you* have a car that doesn't have air-con?' Morton questioned.

'It used to be my sister's car. My parents got her a brand-new Merc, so she doesn't need it anymore. As they didn't like the amount they were offered to trade it in, they gave it to me. It's an acceptable little run-around... When we're not in a heatwave,' Emma-Leigh explained.

As this answered his question, Morton didn't speak again for the rest of the journey.

Mackenzie also didn't speak for the rest of the journey, but she had many questions running through her head. They just weren't ones Emma-Leigh could answer. It was possible that Morton couldn't answer them either, but she was considering asking him them.

—

Upon arrival at Colchester Zoo, which, as Mackenzie discovered, was just a few minutes outside of town down a B road, Emma-Leigh was directed by a marshal to a field. Another marshal pointed to a spot between a Ford S-Max and a large patch of mud.

'Do they not have a proper car park?' Mackenzie questioned.

'They do, but at peak times it's not big enough. This is one of the most popular attractions in Essex. If you're local, then you get used to having to dump your car in the mud. There's an offer on tickets, so that's probably why it's so busy,' Emma-Leigh explained.

The word "local" in Emma-Leigh's sentence intensified Mackenzie's constant wish to be somewhere where *she* was a local.

Taking care not to slip in the mud, Morton eased out of the Clio and then tipped his seat forward to let Mackenzie out.

'Would you like a hand?' Morton asked, not yet holding out his hand.

'No. I can get out of a car by myself,' Mackenzie replied.

A smile appeared on Morton's face as he said: 'I knew you'd say that.'

Just as she had claimed, Mackenzie was able to escape Emma-Leigh's car without assistance. Once she had, she slammed the door, and Emma-Leigh locked the car.

Like dozens of other people, Emma-Leigh, Morton, and Mackenzie trudged across the field full of cars and up a driveway. They all queued, showed their phone screens to people, and were let through barriers by staff.

Once in the zoo itself, Morton unfurled a map he'd picked up.

'Don't you start planning out our entire day! This is supposed to be fun! Spontaneous! We'll just wander around and see things in whatever order we see them,' Emma-Leigh said.

Pointing to some information below the map, Morton replied: 'That sounds... It's fine, if that's how you wish to do things. We should... Perha... You might want to head over to the sea lions first. They're being fed in a few minutes.'

'Oh, yes! Cecilia took Jude here last summer, and she told me the sea lion show was great!' Emma-Leigh agreed.

With her destination decided, Emma-Leigh strode off.

As there were no enclosures that interested her between the entrance and the sea lions, Emma-Leigh kept up quite a pace. This meant that Mackenzie and Morton dropped behind a bit without her noticing.

'How is your new job going?' Morton asked.

After a glance ahead to ensure Emma-Leigh was far enough in front to not quite be in earshot, Mackenzie replied: 'It's difficult to say. I took the job because my mum thinks my uncle is stealing from my grandad's business, and she wanted me to check. From what I've seen, he might be, but he also might just be forgetting to keep track of stock. I told Mum what I've found so far, and she's assumed uncle Eddie is indeed a thief. I'm not sure he is though. I'm not sure of many things right now.'

It struck Morton that Mackenzie had just shared something very important with him. The only person who shared things like that with him was Jude, and not very often. Most of the time, their conversation was light, and there wasn't much of it. He couldn't remember someone sharing a problem with him like Mackenzie just had, and he didn't know how to respond to it.

Before Morton could work out how to support Mackenzie, they reached the sea lion enclosure. Panel after panel of glass looked out onto deep water with some pale rocks at the edge. Most of those panels had people in front of them, looking out into the water.

Emma-Leigh lead her friends around the corner formed by the wall of windows to an empty section. As the sea lions were below the surface of the water, which was reflective, it was difficult to see them, even from a prime spot right in front of a window.

'They can hold their breath for between eight and twenty minutes. That's how they're able to stay under,' Morton explained without being asked to.

'Yes, and they're fun to watch when the keeper throws fish for them, apparently,' Emma-Leigh replied.

So she could record the fun spectacle of sea lions being fed, Emma-Leigh removed her phone from her pocket. When she unlocked the phone, she noticed a red dot by the icon for Facebook. She couldn't leave social media notifications unchecked, so she opened the app and started scrolling.

Taking the opportunity while Emma-Leigh was distracted, Morton leaned in to Mackenzie and whispered: 'Sorry for asking about your job. I was trying to be polite. I didn't mean to remind you of a stressful situation.'

Mackenzie shook her head. 'Don't worry about it. I was already thinking about it, as well as several other things. My head is so full right now,' she murmured into Morton's ear.

Unbeknownst to Mackenzie and Morton, Emma-Leigh had

looked up from her phone for a second while waiting for it to load and spotted the pair of them whispering to each other. '*Yes, that's great! They're sharing something they don't want me to hear. I wonder if what they're saying is sweet or sexual,*' she thought.

After a few seconds of silence, Mackenzie realised she hadn't actually *said* that the situation with her uncle and the family firm was stressful. Morton had worked out by himself how it was affecting her.

From a gate inside the enclosure, a keeper appeared with a bucket in her hand that shone in the sunshine. The murmurs in the crowd grew louder in anticipation of the show. The sleek grey body of a sea lion broke the surface, probably in anticipation of food.

'Good morning, everyone! I'm Sara, and I'm one of the keepers here at Colchester Zoo. I'll be feeding the sea lions today,' the woman with the bucket told everyone, her voice amplified by speakers.

From by a window outside the enclosure, Emma-Leigh pressed record on her phone just in time to capture two more sea lions making their presence known.

Gesturing at the sea lion who'd been first on scene, Sara told the crowd: 'This here is Kerri, who loves to perform.'

Everyone in the crowd except Mackenzie and Morton laughed when Sara threw a fish for Kerri and she darted forward to gulp it down before it had hit the ground.

So they didn't feel left out, Sara threw fish for the other sea lions.

After adjusting her face-mic, Sara declared: 'Right, now Kerri, Karon, and Kayla have had their starter, let's get on with the show.'

Sara had the sea lions perform a variety of tricks, told the audience some facts about them (including that they can hold their breath for a really long time), and fed them plenty of fish.

For the duration of the show, Emma-Leigh did not take her eyes off her phone screen.

It wasn't just the animals that Morton watched. He kept glancing across at Mackenzie, who wasn't reacting to any of the amazing things the sea lions were doing, or the interesting information Sara was providing. It was as if Mackenzie wasn't actually there.

During the show, Sara the zookeeper had mentioned there was a tunnel under the enclosure. When Emma-Leigh suggested to Mackenzie and Morton that they all check it out, they didn't disagree (Mackenzie didn't even answer), so she led them away from the enclosure.

At the bottom of a steep hill was the entrance to the tunnel. There was one door to go in, and one to come out. Mackenzie didn't see this, as she was looking at her ballet pumps.

As they walked through the entrance door, Morton and Emma-Leigh heard a recorded voice explaining the water cycle to all those in earshot who were paying attention.

The only voice Mackenzie heard was her inner voice, questioning the motives of many different people.

'Are you claustrophobic, Mackenzie?' Emma-Leigh asked.

'What?' questioned Mackenzie. A second later, she realised what Emma-Leigh had asked and replied: 'No. I don't mind tight spaces.'

Emma-Leigh nodded.

When she was able to catch Morton's eye, Emma-Leigh beckoned him over.

Distracted by a sea lion swimming right over the thick glass tunnel she was now in, Mackenzie didn't notice that Emma-Leigh and Morton had paused behind her.

'Is it just me, or is something up with Mackenzie? She's seemed distant since we got here,' Emma-Leigh asked Morton in a whisper.

'I've been thinking the same. If *I* am looking at someone and wondering if they're okay, I think that's a sure sign that they very much are not,' Morton hissed back.

'Why the emphasis on "I"? You're good at reading people?' Emma-Leigh questioned quietly.

In response, Morton raised an eyebrow.

'Okay, I lied out of politeness. You're *not* good at reading people. Neither am I, sometimes. It's hard,' Emma-Leigh admitted.

Ahead of Emma-Leigh and Morton, Mackenzie was gazing at her own reflection. With a jolt, she remembered she wasn't alone and turned to face the people she'd gone to the zoo with.

'Sorry. I was just... Erm... I was wondering how thick this glass is. I know it's sad that I'm more interested in the construction of this thing than the animals you can see through it. My only excuse is that I'm an architect. Well, I have a degree in architecture. I've never actually worked *as* an architect, though I have worked *with* architects,' Mackenzie rambled.

'It's ten centimetres thick, to hold back five-hundred-thousand gallons,' Morton revealed.

'What?' Mackenzie questioned.

Gesturing at the tunnel walls, Morton said: 'The glass is ten centimetres thick. A moment ago, you were wondering how thick it is. At least, you *said* you were wondering. I know that's *not* what was on your mind. What *was* on your mind, I do *not* know, but I bet it's nothing to do with your surroundings.'

For the first time, Mackenzie properly took in her surroundings. It was an incredible feat of engineering, designed to allow visitors to view the sea lions in the enclosure above. It was somewhere to be admired in awe. It wasn't somewhere to share secrets.

'I didn't sleep well, that's all. I'll try to focus from now on,' Mackenzie lied.

Emma-Leigh clapped her hands together. 'Right then. In that case, I think we should head to the coffee shop. I've had many a sleepless night, some things are more important than sleep when you're with someone as hot as Ronnie, and I find that coffee and cake always perks me up,' she said.

'But... That's not... Not... It's not...' Morton stammered.

'I think what you're trying to say is that it isn't lunchtime yet. Don't worry about it. We can have this and then something else later. Anyway, let's get to the coffee shop,' Emma-Leigh interrupted.

The idea of moving on, physically and mentally, sounded great to Mackenzie. 'Yes, let's get on,' she agreed, striding off down the tunnel even though she didn't know where the coffee shop was.

As she followed Mackenzie with Morton, Emma-Leigh hissed to him: 'Yes, I know it's rude to finish someone's sentence for them when they're stuttering, but I didn't want you to say what you were trying to say. You're right that what's wrong with Mackenzie is more than a bad night's sleep, but she obviously doesn't want to talk about it here. There's nothing we can do except try to distract her.'

After Morton told Mackenzie that, despite living in the desert, meerkats don't drink because they get all the water they need from their diet, and that leaf-cutter ants only live for six to ten weeks, Emma-Leigh regretted saying that they should try to distract Mackenzie. She regretted it even more when Morton started to explain that, if you take size into account, the cheetah *isn't* the fastest land animal.

While dragging herself through the zoo listening to an endless list of facts, Emma-Leigh thought: *'This is going to be a long day, and not like what I'd planned. Instead of Mackenzie and Morton getting closer and falling in love in front of my very eyes, she's just shut herself off, from him and everyone. Now, not only do I not get to crow about another great match made, but I have to put up with Morton at his most boring while trying to work out how to get Mackenzie to open up.'*

Chapter Twenty-nine

As soon as Emma-Leigh pulled away from Mr Wight's house having just dropped Mackenzie off, she asked Morton: 'Are you doing anything tonight?'

Morton laughed. 'What do you think? As I'm sure you're aware, Jude's having a cosy night in with Cecilia, so he's not available. As you may *not* be aware, Tamsyn is on shift every day this week. If I'm not working, and Jude and Tamsyn *aren't* available, then *I* probably *am* available. The only exception to that is the odd weekend when I go and see my parents, and emergencies,' he replied.

'I'm going to take that as a no then, which is good. Good for Mackenzie at least,' Emma-Leigh said.

As he knew Emma-Leigh would explain why it was good that he was available, Morton didn't ask any questions.

A pedestrian walking out in front of her demanded all of Emma-Leigh's attention and temporarily prevented her from revealing her plans to Morton.

Once she was on a quieter street, Emma-Leigh explained: 'You should take Mackenzie out to a restaurant. I'm sure she'd open up to you in a place like that. I'd take her out myself, but I've got plans. Jude and Cecilia aren't the only couple staying in tonight, but my night with Ronnie will probably be more *steamy* than *cosy*. Besides, she might prefer to talk to you than me. She's spent more time with you, and I know she likes you.'

Part of Morton wanted to ask *how* Emma-Leigh knew Mackenzie liked him. As it wasn't relevant, he didn't. Mackenzie's welfare was more important than his curiosity.

'There is an issue with your plan. Mackenzie won't want to go out to dinner tonight. Definitely not with me,' Morton pointed out.

'I've already come up with a little white lie to get her out of the house. The story is that Jude messaged you to say that he and Cecilia have a table booked at Tricia's. Neither of them really want to go out, but Cecilia won't cancel because she feels bad about letting the restaurant down. Jude really wants a night in, and he's asked you, his best friend, if you can take someone to Tricia's. That way, the restaurant will still have two diners at that time, so Cecilia can stay home without feeling bad. As Mackenzie owes Jude a favour for borrowing his car, she's sure to agree,' Emma-Leigh replied.

Before he gave his answer, Morton thoroughly considered the details of the lie. It all seemed to make sense. If he was Mackenzie, he'd believe it and, as Emma-Leigh said, he'd go along with it to thank Jude for the use of his car.

'Yes, it works. I'll do it,' Morton agreed.

'Great!' Emma-Leigh cried.

To stop himself from commenting on how bad Emma-Leigh's attempt at parallel parking was, Morton wondered what to do if he couldn't get Mackenzie to tell him what was wrong. He'd been given a task without any instructions on how to complete it, or even a rulebook. That was his idea of a nightmare.

30

Chapter Thirty

A note on the winged armchair in the lounge told Mackenzie that her grandad, who would usually be sat in that chair at that time, was next door teaching Hazel how to use her new Kindle. When she read where Mr Wight was, she sighed.

As Emma-Leigh was paid to clean once a week, Mr Wight's house was spotless. This left Mackenzie with very little housework she could do to distract herself from worrying and wondering about many different things.

When she looked down at her baby blue blouse, which she'd got chocolate icing on whilst at the zoo, it occurred to Mackenzie that Emma-Leigh didn't do the washing. Getting some pale tops together to throw in the machine could keep her occupied for ten minutes or so.

Without reading the labels on her tops, or considering the spin speed, Mackenzie chose a setting on the washing machine that would make it run at forty degrees for just over an hour. It only took her six minutes.

The whirr of the washing machine kept Mackenzie company as she sat in the lounge and scrolled through Facebook. Reading about acquaintances of hers pretending their lives were perfect just about stopped her from going next door and making up an excuse for her grandad to come back. She was aware that it wouldn't keep her in her seat for long.

After showing her a video of a sparkling diamond in a silver ring, Mackenzie's phone informed her it was receiving a call from "Morton SNOOKER". A call she accepted.

'Mackenzie! I'm glad you answered. If at all possible, I could do with a favour from you,' Morton said.

'Please want me to do something right now. Anything would be better than sitting here, going over every decision I've ever made, and every decision I have not made,' Mackenzie thought to herself.

'I may be able to help,' Mackenzie said to Morton.

'Would you go out for dinner with me tonight, to a restaurant in town?' Morton asked.

That wasn't what Mackenzie had expected Morton to ask her to do. She'd thought that maybe he needed a lift, or money. Perhaps a phone call at a certain time to get him out of a boring party. Going for dinner with Morton would keep her out all night. As she wanted to go out for dinner with him, Mackenzie decided not to question why Morton had asked her out.

'What time? Do you need me to get myself to town, or were you planning on picking me up?' Mackenzie questioned.

For a few seconds, there was silence on the line. This was because Morton was struggling to absorb the fact that Mackenzie had agreed to go out with him.

'Erm, eight, but we could get there early if you like. I'd like to get a taxi together into town. I wasn't expecting you to get there yourself, though I know you're fully capable. It's just that, as long as it doesn't offend you, I'd like to accompany you. One of my friends is a paramedic, we sometimes talk about her work, and what she tells me scares me. I don't like being alone outside after dark,' Morton replied.

It made Mackenzie smile that Morton knew him not wanting her to go into town alone might offend her. He seemed to know her inside out. A voice in her head told her he knew her better than she knew herself at that moment in time.

'I understand, and would be quite happy to share a cab. Any time from now is fine by me. I'm not with anyone or doing anything,' Mackenzie told Morton.

When he found out Mackenzie was unoccupied and alone, Morton said: 'I'll get there as soon as possible.'

Chapter Thirty-one

As the driver moaned for the whole drive about the "drunken ex-army lot" that "littered" Colchester's streets, Mackenzie didn't speak during the taxi ride into town.

When she and Morton were dropped off outside Tricia's, Mackenzie handed the driver a note and told him: 'I'm sure some, if not all of, the people who were brave enough to serve our country and now find themselves sleeping rough would much rather be in a safe and warm home than "littering the streets". I *know* that I'd rather give them this money than you.'

'If you did, they'd only spend it on alcohol, or drugs. You're supposed to give it to a charity that supports them, like Shelter or The Sally Army, if you really want to spend your hard-earned cash on that sort,' the taxi driver pointed out.

As she knew the taxi driver was right that those who wanted to support homeless people and rough sleepers were supposed to give money to charity instead of directly to someone sitting on the street, Mackenzie didn't answer.

When the taxi driver started his engine to drive off, *then* Mackenzie had something to say. 'I didn't tell you to keep the change,' she pointed out.

In response, the taxi driver shoved the 60p he owed Mackenzie into her outstretched hand. With that done, he and his company-owned Skoda screeched off down the road.

To Mackenzie's right, Morton was grinning. 'You're so bold and brave,' he said.

'I wish,' Mackenzie murmured.

Morton considered insisting that Mackenzie *was* bold and brave. He decided against it, as it would only lead to conversational tennis with her repeatedly denying it, forcing him to affirm it again and again. Instead, he said: 'At least he dropped us off right outside. Let's go in and get settled.'

The restaurant was on the corner of the street. Mackenzie couldn't tell whether it had been there thirty years, or two-hundred-and-thirty years. When she entered the building with Morton, she was confronted by a man with a tablet.

'Good evening, Sir, Madam. What is your name, Sir?' the tablet-wielding man asked.

'Morton Lowe. I have booked a table,' Morton replied.

To check this, the waiter briefly glanced down at his tablet. When he saw what he wanted to see, he let it hang by the silver strap that was across his body and matched his tie. 'Of course, Sir. If you would be so kind as to follow me with your companion, we can get you seated,' he told Morton.

As she walked through the building to the back, Mackenzie glanced around her at other people's plates. Either everyone she'd looked at had almost finished, or the portions were tiny.

Once he had seated Morton and Mackenzie, the waiter told them: 'The sommelier will be over shortly to take your drinks order. You will find the food menus in front of you on the table.'

Having done his duty, the waiter returned to the entrance.

After looking around himself to make sure none of the staff were in earshot, Morton said: 'Would now be a good time to point out that Emma-Leigh recommended this place?'

'Ah, now that makes sense. Why did you ask Emma-Leigh of all people to recommend a restaurant, and what inspired you to take me out?' Mackenzie questioned.

Morton blushed. 'I didn't exactly *ask* her. On the drive from your home to mine, we talked about you and how distant you'd been. It's obvious, to us at least, that you've got a lot on your mind. Stuff you may wish to share. She couldn't ask you out herself, because she's staying home with Ronnie. It sounds like they're going to have lots of sex, so I can understand why she won't change her plans. She came up with this convoluted lie about Jude and Cecilia booking a table they don't want, and him asking me to go to the restaurant with someone so he didn't have to. You may have noticed that I didn't tell you this lie when I called you to ask you out. I thought about it, but it seemed silly. As it was, you came out anyway. Now, you can share whatever is in your head with me, if you want to,' he explained.

A lump formed in Mackenzie's throat when she thought about Emma-Leigh and Morton discussing how to help her. It reminded her of her parents and sister back in Sheffield. All of them had at times noticed she was down, and helped in their own ways. She could picture her dad walking into her room one day when she was fifteen, sitting on her bed, and asking what was wrong. On that occasion, she'd been stressed about exams. Support was something she'd come to expect from her family, and one of the many things she'd loved about Shaun was that he listened to her worries, but no friends of hers had ever worked together to help her in that way.

Unbeknownst to Mackenzie, she stared into space for well over ten seconds. Morton, who had no idea what was on her mind, deduced that he must have done something wrong. 'I'm sorry we talked about you behind your back. We had good intentions, I promise,' he said.

The sadness in Morton's voice dragged Mackenzie from Sheffield in the past to present-day Colchester. 'I know you two did. I'm just stunned that you're so kind. You know listening to me going on won't be fun, don't you?' she questioned.

'Yes, but it doesn't have to be fun. Friendship is not all about *fun*. If it was, then I wouldn't be so lucky as to have three people who I can call my friends,' Morton pointed out.

'As one of those three friends, I can tell you that I've had a lot of fun with you at times, and I'm as lucky to have you as you are to have me,' Mackenzie replied.

As he didn't know how to answer such a sweet compliment, Morton was pleased to see the sommelier approaching them.

Handing him an A4 sheet of paper with the words "WINE LIST" at the top, the sommelier told Morton: 'This is the wine list.'

Immediately after the sommelier had given Morton the wine list, he gave it to Mackenzie. 'I don't drink wine,' he explained.

The sommelier frowned. 'You are going to let your female companion choose?' he questioned.

Morton's "female companion" scanned the wine list. The various options had been arranged alphabetically. Mackenzie ignored the titles and long descriptions. They were meaningless to her. To make her choice, she searched the column of prices for the second-lowest number.

Pointing to one of the red wines, Mackenzie told the sommelier: 'I'll have a bottle of that.'

'A fine choice. It pairs well with the steak,' the sommelier declared.

Neither Morton nor Mackenzie had anything to say about her choice of wine. The idea of eating steak made Mackenzie's mouth water, but she didn't need to tell the sommelier that.

When he realised his customers weren't going to thank him for approving of their choice of wine, the sommelier wondered what sort of thing Morton drank. '*I bet he's the sort who drinks Jägerbombs,*' the sommelier thought to himself.

'Can I have a vodka and cola?' Morton asked.

The sommelier recoiled. 'No. We don't serve that sort of thing here. We *do* have an extensive list of quality cocktails,' he replied.

'I'll just have lemonade, thanks,' Morton said.

'Ah, now that we *do* have. We have the finest Sicilian lemonade, which I shall bring you a glass of with the lady's wine,' the sommelier told Morton.

After taking the wine list back from Mackenzie, the sommelier pranced off to the bar.

As soon as the sommelier was out of earshot, Morton and Mackenzie burst out laughing. This drew the attention of a few of their fellow diners, but neither of them noticed.

'Is it just me, or is this place *fake* posh? I swear he doesn't know a thing about wine, except for a couple of facts he picked up from Google. He just makes out that he does, and frowns on people who want normal drinks to give the impression that this is a restaurant with a reputation to uphold,' Mackenzie asked.

Morton nodded. 'I agree,' he agreed.

When he thought about what drinks had been ordered, Morton wondered if a mistake had been made. 'Will you be alright with a whole bottle of wine to yourself?' he asked.

'I'll need every last drop. It's difficult for me to accept help. The wine should relax me,' Mackenzie replied.

Silence fell at Mackenzie and Morton's table, and at many other tables. They both decided to take the opportunity to read their menus.

When she read the menu, Mackenzie realised what simple taste she had in food. There was only one thing she was prepared to eat. Thankfully, it was something she'd wanted since before opening the menu. Her menu didn't have prices on, so she had no idea how expensive it was. As long as Morton let her pay, money wasn't an issue.

Opposite Mackenzie, Morton was pondering what adventure to take his taste buds on. Going to a restaurant that he would never have chosen gave him an opportunity to eat something that wasn't on the menus of the places he usually went.

As they both decided what they wanted, Morton and Mackenzie closed their menus simultaneously.

A few seconds later, a waitress brought a bottle of wine and a glass of lemonade over on a black plastic tray. Standing in between Morton and Mackenzie, the waitress plonked both drinks on the table.

'I'm Pixie Lynch, and I'll be your waitress for the evening. Enjoy!' the waitress said.

'Could we order some food, please?' Morton asked.

Pixie grinned. 'Of course. What would you like?' she replied.

'The salmon en croûte, I think,' Morton said.

'A pretty fishy dishy,' Pixie commented.

It was then that Mackenzie realised Pixie didn't have a notepad or a tablet. All she had was a stain on her silver waistcoat and a beaming smile. Both seemed at odds with the ambiance of the restaurant.

'And I'll have the steak. Rare, please,' Mackenzie told the smiley and untidy waitress.

'An uncommon post with a pointy end coming right up,' Pixie replied.

When she saw the confused look on Mackenzie's face, the waitress giggled. 'Yes, I know that stake as in something you kill a vampire with is spelt differently from steak that's a bit of cow which you eat, and you meant rare as in "not cooked much", but it makes me laugh, so I have to say it,' she explained.

Something about Pixie made Mackenzie feel warm inside, like everything might just be okay.

'Saying silly things helps me remember people's orders. Also, it makes them smile, which in a place like this is a miracle,' Pixie revealed.

'Won't you get in trouble for this?' Morton asked.

Pixie giggled again. 'Oh, yes! I'm on a final warning. I may even be fired tonight. So what? I'm on minimum wage, *literally* minimum wage as I'm only nineteen. There are dozens of eateries in Colchester. By next weekend, I'll have another job. A better one too,' she replied.

With that, Pixie skipped away to the kitchen.

'I remember being that carefree,' Mackenzie commented wistfully.

'Now is the time to share with me what it is you're caring so much about,' Morton pointed out.

After filling her wine glass and then downing most of it, Mackenzie replied: 'No, *now* is the time.'

32

Chapter Thirty-two

At first, Mackenzie spoke slowly, with many gaps to gather her thoughts. As the wine bottle emptied, she spoke faster, with fewer pauses and more emotion.

While listening to Mackenzie, Morton made non-committal sounds to encourage her to continue. A communication course he'd once taken online had said this made the speaker feel heard. That same course told him he should repeat someone's words back to them, to prove he had listened and understood. As Mackenzie had been talking for almost an hour, it was impossible to repeat everything. Morton decided to summarise what he'd heard.

'So, your cheater ex-boyfriend helped your sister, and you can't understand why he did it? Once upon a time, you'd have expected such behaviour from Shaun, but now you know he cheated, and you've had huge rows about that, it seems strange that he'd do something so nice?' Morton questioned.

'Yes! Exactly that!' Mackenzie cried.

After downing the last of her wine, straight from the bottle,

Mackenzie said: 'He hates me, but he acts like he loves me. I love him, but I hate him for what he did to me. It's all such a mess! I would think he rescued Brit to make it up to me that he cheated, but to this day, he's adamant that he *didn't* cheat. It's all just going around and around in my head.'

Morton sighed. 'Goodness knows why he did what he did. I'm sorry to say that you'll probably never know. I have a million theories, but they wouldn't help. I do have a feeling that he *doesn't* hate you. I can't give you an answer,' he told Mackenzie.

'Don't worry about it. I just needed to share. I can't tell anyone about this. My family think I'm over him, my Sheffield friends were never that good with things like this and I've lost touch with them anyway, and I can't tell Emma-Leigh because she'll think Shaun *does* love me and I should get over what he did and get back with him,' Mackenzie rambled.

The waitress who'd visited Mackenzie and Morton's table an hour ago returned with two plates of food, which she placed in front of them. 'This *is* my last night. I've been "respectfully asked not to return", for too many offenses to list. It backfired on them though, because I may have just let slip that I saw the maître d' take a two-hundred-pound tip which he didn't share,' Pixie revealed.

Mackenzie laughed. 'You go, girl!' she replied.

'Yes, I will, and not come back. It feels wonderful!' Pixie said.

When Pixie tried to walk away, Mackenzie asked: 'Could I have some more wine?'

Pixie, who was already ten feet or so away, called back: 'Sure. I'll send the wine guy.'

Looking at his slither of salmon wrapped in pastry, Morton wondered how it could be worth what he was going to have to pay for it.

'Generous, aren't they(?)' Mackenzie remarked sarcastically.

'It's probably part of the fake posh thing. Fancy restaurants famously serve small portions,' Morton replied.

After eating her small portion of quite fatty steak and undercooked chips, washed down with wine, Mackenzie realised how much lighter she felt than she had at the start of the day. It was nothing to do with the food and everything to do with Morton and Malbec.

As both his plate and Mackenzie's were empty, Morton decided to try to strike up a light conversation. 'So, you live with your grandparents?' he asked.

'My *grandad*, Dad's dad. My grandmother left Grandad a couple of years ago,' Mackenzie replied.

'Oh, I'm sorry to hear that,' Morton said.

'Yeah, so was Grandad when his wife of over forty years says she doesn't love him anymore and files for divorce,' Mackenzie revealed.

Morton's mouth fell open. 'Oh, I thought she'd *died*. I didn't know people got divorced at that age,' he told Mackenzie.

'Yes, it came as quite a shock to my Grandad, and pretty much the whole family. We suspect she found someone else, but we'll probably never know for sure. She went after his business, but she didn't manage to get her mitts on it,' Mackenzie revealed.

As he adjusted his shirt collar, Morton wondered how his attempt at light conversation had failed so spectacularly. He went on to wonder if it was *necessary* for conversation to be light.

Seeing that her glass was empty, Mackenzie poured herself more wine. The moment her glass was full, she put the bottle down and took a sip from it. Having had many sips of wine by that point, she didn't taste it, or notice the warm sensation as it travelled down her body.

'The worst thing about my grandparents splitting up is it leaves Grandad lonely and vulnerable. The next-door neighbour is trying to worm her way into his life at the moment. I have not worked out why yet, but no doubt she wants something from Grandad, and she's taking advantage of the fact that he's sad, and old, and alone. The thing is, he's not alone. He's got me. A bit like the work thing though, with my uncle, I can't be sure Hazel's up to no good, so I can't do anything. At least, I don't think I can. It's up to me to look after Grandad, and his business, and to try to work out what the hell is going on with Shaun, but I'm not sure about any of it. I've got no idea if I'm doing the right thing or not. I've got to make decisions, but with no facts or figures or evidence to base them on,' Mackenzie rambled.

By now, Morton understood why Mackenzie had been so distant. 'I question every decision I make which isn't based on facts, unless it concerns snooker. It sounds like you're doing the same, and you're facing a lot of decisions at the moment. You've got a lot to question right now. No wonder you're struggling,' he commented.

The words "no wonder you're struggling" hit a nerve. For much of the trip around the zoo, Mackenzie had been berating herself for feeling stressed and tired. Now, she felt justified. It was okay to not be okay.

When tears started falling from Mackenzie's eyes, she didn't care. Releasing them in the form of water was simply the natural thing to do with her feelings.

As he *did* care, Morton got up to wrap Mackenzie in a hug.

Being held by a man who'd let her share her feelings brought back memories for Mackenzie. At that moment, in Morton's arms, she wondered if he was Essex's non-cheating version of Shaun. She wondered if she loved him.

When Mackenzie's tears dried up, Morton returned to his seat.

'Drink always makes me well up. That's why I don't ever have much,' Mackenzie told Morton.

'It makes me even more boring. I know that sounds impossible, but it isn't. Alcohol is not a one-size-fits-all thing. It affects different people in very different ways. Arguably, some of those people shouldn't drink it,' Morton revealed.

It occurred to Mackenzie that was one of the few things she'd learnt about Morton that night. 'Tell me more about you. We've gone on about me all night, which was the point, but I'm feeling guilty now. I'd like to know something more about you,' she said.

'I have a stammer. That's something you should know about me. It only tends to show these days when I'm stressed, but in secondary school I stammered all the time. As you can imagine, some of my fellow pupils decided this was an excuse to pick on me. Were it not for a certain Jude Austen, who mocked my bullies and never spoke for me, even if it took me ten minutes to finish a sentence, I probably wouldn't have made it through. It is thanks to him that I'm where I am today,' Morton told Mackenzie.

For a moment, Mackenzie thought she might cry again. 'That's incredible! I had no idea about your stammer, or that Jude meant so much to you!' she cried.

'He's a good man. Not just for being friends with me. He quietly supports so many people. Even more so since he met Cecilia,' Morton commented.

As happy as Mackenzie was that Jude and Cecilia had found each other and were very much in love, she didn't want to talk about it. It made her jealous.

Thinking about jealousy brought to mind the five-hundred-and-eighty-four-thousand or so people who got to call Sheffield home. She yearned to still be one of them. It prompted a question for Morton. 'Have you always lived here?' she asked him.

Just before Morton told Mackenzie exactly where he came from, it occurred to him that she wouldn't know anything about the place. Telling her its name would be pointless. 'I was born and raised in a little Essex village. I moved to town because I got tired of not being able to have fresh fruit and vegetables every day without driving,' he replied.

What Morton said about not being able to get fruit and veg confused Mackenzie. 'What do you mean? Were you on a country lane between villages, so unable to walk to the shops?' she questioned.

'Shop, *singular*, and I lived across the road from it. I could walk there, and often did. It's just that they didn't stock much fresh produce. The fresh produce they *did* sell, they'd order so little of it that they'd often run out. They even ran out of bread and milk on twenty-two occasions,' Morton explained.

Mackenzie gasped. 'What a funny place you grew up in!' she cried.

That response told Morton that Mackenzie was a city girl through and through. He didn't need to ask if she'd lived in Sheffield her whole life. It was obvious. He was willing to bet she hadn't even been on holiday somewhere that didn't have at the very least a selection of takeaways that delivered to where she was staying.

When Morton saw the waiter who had greeted him and Mackenzie when they'd arrived coming over, he sighed.

'Would Sir and Madam care for the dessert menu?' the waiter asked when he got to Morton.

'No, not really. "Madam" would like the bill,' Mackenzie replied, using her fingers to make quotation marks in the air.

The waiter blushed. 'Of course. Right away,' he said before bowing his head and scuttling away.

Not for the first time after a visit from a member of the restaurant's staff, Morton and Mackenzie burst out laughing.

'You think I'm bold when I'm *sober*. Look what I can do when I'm a bit tipsy,' Mackenzie said.

Though he thought Mackenzie was more than "a bit tipsy", he decided not to correct her.

There was silence until the waiter returned with the card

machine, which he placed in front of Morton. He'd also brought over a silver dish with a white sticker on it that had "TIPS" written on it in marker pen. 'If the amount is correct, insert your card, type your PIN number, and we can get this all paid for you,' the waiter ordered.

'The N of PIN stands for number, therefore it is unnecessary and incorrect to say "PIN number". It's a tautology,' Morton pointed out.

After correcting the waiter, Morton reached for his wallet.

Before Morton could even get into his coat pocket, Mackenzie thrust her hand over the card machine. 'Don't you dare, Luke Rattigan! I'm paying this,' she told Morton.

The waiter frowned, but said nothing. He had finally learnt not to question anything Mackenzie did.

'Firstly, I love the niche Doctor Who reference. Secondly, I asked you out, so I should pay,' Morton argued.

'Nope, not tonight. Not with me. Usually, I'd agree that if you ask someone out, you should pay. If, however, the person you've asked out is a multimillionaire, like me, and you are *not* a multimillionaire, then it is only fair that they pay,' Mackenzie replied.

When he realised he was serving a multimillionaire, the waiter started dreaming about the suit he'd buy with the massive tip he was surely about to receive.

The look on Morton's face told Mackenzie he was too shocked to speak. She could understand. What *do* you say when you find out your friend is loaded?

To make things easier for Morton, Mackenzie decided to tell him how she'd got her fortune. 'I won a lottery. I got *millions*. Most of it is sitting around in a savings account. I still haven't got used to the fact that I'm rich,' she explained.

Still, Morton couldn't form words for a response.

Ignoring Morton, the waiter gave Mackenzie the card machine.

'Congratulations! I'm honoured that you chose to spend some of your winnings here,' he said.

As she inserted her card and typed her PIN, Mackenzie told the waiter: 'I *didn't* choose to come here. Morton brought me, and it was recommended to him by a friend with questionable taste.'

It amused Mackenzie to see the waiter's cheeks turn red. The harsh manner in which he ripped the receipt off the card machine and thrust it into her hand made her want to roar with laughter.

Gesturing at the silver "TIPS" dish, the waiter said: 'Leave whatever you like in here. If you wish to pay card, that's fine. The machine would have asked if you'd like to add a gratuity, but you may have missed that. Anything is appreciated.'

After finding out Pixie had been fired, Mackenzie had known exactly how much she was going to tip the restaurant. It gave her immense pleasure to get her clutch bag off the floor, open it with great care, remove a few 20p coins that had been given to her by the rude taxi driver, and place them in the "TIPS" dish.

With a smile on her face that gave her dimples and lit up her eyes, Mackenzie rose from her seat and said to Morton: 'Let's go.'

33

Chapter Thirty-three

For most of the taxi ride home, Mackenzie told the driver about how strange Tricia's was. When she told him she'd left a 60p tip (she didn't mention that she'd won a lottery), the driver laughed.

'Dear me! You don't take kindly to bad service, do you? I hope I don't receive the same treatment,' the driver said.

Mackenzie shook her head. There was a delay between her moving her head, and her field of vision moving. It was so disorientating that she couldn't speak for a few moments.

'Don't worry. This isn't bad service, so I'll be nice,' Mackenzie eventually told the driver.

Safe in the knowledge that Mackenzie would be nice to him, and amused by how much she was slurring, the driver continued to not provide bad service and got her and Morton safely to their destination.

The moment the taxi stopped, Morton jumped out and dashed round to Mackenzie's side. He opened the door and held out his hand for her to hold. When he saw the frown on Mackenzie's face, Morton pointed out: 'I know you wouldn't usually want help, but you're inebriated and wearing high heels. If you fall and hurt yourself, then you'll need help from lots of people. This is the better option.'

'I've nattered on at you for hours, so I have already accepted your help. Taking your hand is nothing. Besides, I'm tipsy now, so I don't care,' Mackenzie replied.

To get out of the car, Mackenzie seized Morton's hand and swung both her legs out, planting her feet firmly on the floor. As she stood mere millimetres from Morton, gazing into his eyes, she noticed that she felt woozy and slightly nauseous. Her heart hammered away in her chest. '*I feel very weird. This must be love. Morton is a nice lad. I must be in love with him,*' she thought.

'Let's get to the house,' Mackenzie said.

As Morton wanted to get Mackenzie into her house, he didn't disagree. He just linked arms with her and started walking down the drive to the front door.

'Don't feel like you have to rush. This is a quiet time of night. I'm happy to wait as long as you need,' the taxi driver called to Morton.

Stumbling down her grandad's driveway clinging on to Morton's arm, the feelings Mackenzie had first noticed when she'd got out the car intensified.

When he and Mackenzie reached her front door, Morton released her arm so she could get her key out. He was confident that she could remain upright unaided while stationary.

After fishing her key out of her clutch bag, Mackenzie's gaze met Morton's. A few seconds later, it lowered to his lips. Warmth flooded through her. In that moment, she knew exactly what she wanted, and it wasn't to open her door.

'What?' Morton asked.

Mackenzie laid a finger on Morton's lips. 'Shush,' she ordered.

In a single second, Mackenzie replaced her finger with her lips, pressing them onto Morton's. He was overcome by her scent, fruity and boozy, with hints of beef. When he adjusted to the smell of her, he became aware of the feel of her lips on his, forceful and demanding. Lost in sensation, Morton wasn't aware of anything but Mackenzie.

In an amount of time Morton was unable to measure, Mackenzie released him and backed off, ending their kiss. A kiss that had left Morton speechless.

The kiss *hadn't* left Mackenzie speechless. *She* was able to say: 'Oh, I don't think I *do* love you. How weird.'

As she had no more plans for Morton, Mackenzie slotted her key into the door and turned it until she heard the familiar "click" sound of the lock disengaging.

Just before she stepped through her front door and parted company with Morton, Mackenzie told him: 'Thanks. I feel so much better for this. Goodnight.'

34

Chapter Thirty-four

Facebook informed Morton that Jude was feeling "in love" and watching *Miss Congeniality*. With this information, Jude had posted: "Cecilia: Sandra Bullock is so beautiful!

Me: Yeah, specially at the end of the film.

Cecilia: Really? I think she is most attractive at the start, when she's her real self.

Both of us: Would dump you to date Sandra Bullock if given the opportunity.

Also both of us: Sandra Bullock is well out of our league, and we're quite happy with each other. Let's just stick with what we've got."

What his best friend was watching was of little interest to Morton. It didn't stop him thinking about Mackenzie kissing him. Most likely, there was nothing on Facebook that could distract him, so he closed the app.

As soon as Morton had put his phone down on the bedside table, it dinged to tell him he'd received a message. Thinking it was odd for someone to message him, especially at that time of night, Morton picked the phone back up and opened Messenger.

The new Facebook message, which was from Emma-Leigh Layton, read: "Saw you were active. How did it go with Mackenzie?"

The first response Morton thought of was: "Well, she planted her lips on mine."

As he didn't want to share news of his kiss with Emma-Leigh, or anyone, Morton reconsidered his message. Summarising an evening of support was challenging, but he worked it out.

"Mackenzie shared with me what's on her mind. There's a lot going on in her life right now. Nothing you need to know or worry about. The restaurant you had us go to was very strange" Morton typed.

As he had to wait for Emma-Leigh's reply, Morton couldn't settle down to sleep. He didn't blame Emma-Leigh for keeping him awake though. Replaying Mackenzie's kiss would probably have done that, and he couldn't help but think of it over and over again.

It didn't take Emma-Leigh long to answer. "Glad Mackenzie is okay. Thanks for your help with that. She's a special girl. I have to know she's okay. You say restaurant strange. What you mean? Was planning to take Ronnie there for anniversary" she told Morton.

The speed of Emma-Leigh's response suggested to Morton that she wasn't doing anything. This surprised him. He thought Ronnie would be keeping her busy.

Smiling as he remembered how Mackenzie had described the restaurant, Morton replied: "Tricia's is fake posh. I would suggest you take Ronnie somewhere else to celebrate your anniversary. Speaking of Ronnie, doesn't he need your attention?"

Before Morton could even open his water bottle to have a sip of drink, Emma-Leigh messaged: "He fell asleep an hour ago."

Even after gulping down half his bottle of water, Morton wasn't sure what to say to Emma-Leigh about the fact that her boyfriend was asleep at 11pm on their couple's night in.

Morton let out a sigh of relief when he saw that Emma-Leigh was typing, so he wouldn't have to comment on her relationship.

"Ta very much for advice about Tricia's, and what you've done for Mackenzie. That's all I wanted from you, so I'm going to go now and let you sleep" Emma-Leigh said.

Having finished his conversation with Emma-Leigh, Morton returned his mobile to its spot on the bedside table and let his head sink into his pillow.

Chapter Thirty-five

When Mackenzie awoke, her head felt like it was made of rock. Based on how her sister had described them, she was experiencing a hangover. It was the first time she'd had one.

Her lack of energy and the unsettled feeling in her tummy made Mackenzie reluctant to move. She may never have been hungover before, but she knew that sudden moves were to be avoided. Drinking water, eating the right food, and taking it slow were all key. As she lay there, the events of the previous night came back to her. Some were hazy, but one she remembered crystal clear.

To an empty house, Mackenzie cried: 'Bollocks! I kissed Morton! Not only did I kiss him, but then I told him I don't love him!'

As soon as Mackenzie remembered kissing Morton, she knew what her task was for the day. That task was to get in touch with Morton, apologise, and not throw up while doing that.

Having failed at the last part of her task, and cleaned up the resulting mess, Mackenzie called Morton's mobile. It rang and rang, and eventually went to voicemail. She left a message asking him to call her when he got that message.

It occurred to Mackenzie that Morton might be working. She didn't know what his job was, or when he did it. She felt very lucky that it was her day off.

When her phone rang, Mackenzie snatched it off the arm of the chair she'd curled up in and answered the call without reading the name on screen. 'Oh, I'm so glad you answered. I am really sorry about kissing you last night,' Mackenzie said.

'Eh? You were hundreds of miles away from me last night, and we've never kissed. I may be into girls, but not girls like you,' a Northern female voice replied.

Only then did it occur to Mackenzie to check the caller ID. She took the phone away from her ear and saw the name "Kathryn Carlisle".

'Why are *you* calling me?' Mackenzie wondered out loud.

'For tourist advice. I'm taking my girlfriend on a city break to London. I hear from Jackie that you're in that neck of the woods now, and I was wondering if you could recommend anywhere I should take her,' Kathryn explained.

Confused, Mackenzie pinched herself. It hurt, which confirmed that she wasn't dreaming. '*Do hangovers send you loopy? Brit's never mentioned that,*' Mackenzie thought.

Having decided that the woman who her ex-boyfriend cheated with really *had* just called her to ask about London, Mackenzie tried to get her aching brain to form a response.

She couldn't think of words to say out loud, but in her head Mackenzie said: '*Cheers, Jackie, for telling Kathy where I moved to. Still, you always were a sweetheart, so I guess you couldn't see the harm in it.*'

'It's the first time I've taken Leigh away, and I want it to be special for her. She likes quiet little cafés and pubs that aren't too poncy or expensive. I know you won the lottery, but, knowing you, it hasn't changed your tastes. Nothing could make you uppity. You must know some good places in London,' Kathryn explained when Mackenzie stayed silent.

'I live in *Colchester*! London is two hours away on the train,' Mackenzie pointed out. Stating facts was all she felt able to do.

'Oh, sorry. Down South is all the same to me,' Kathryn said.

'Interesting that you'll apologise for not realising that London and Colchester are completely different places, but *not* for sleeping with Shaun. *My* Shaun at the time,' Mackenzie blurted out. Suddenly her brain had fired up. The angry and hurt part of it at least.

'That'd be because I didn't. He's a man. Why would *I* want him?' Kathryn replied.

The whole room started to spin, or at least that's how it looked to Mackenzie. She dropped her phone on the chair behind her and ran to the toilet.

When Mackenzie returned to the lounge, she was surprised to see that Kathryn was still on the line.

'What was that? Are you alright?' Kathryn questioned.

'I was just chucking my guts up. I'm hungover. I got very drunk last night, partly in an attempt to block the pain of what you and Shaun did. I loved that man, I still *do* love that man, and you took him away from me,' Mackenzie replied.

'Erm, no I didn't. Don't you know I'm a lesbian? I thought the whole city did. Whatever made you think that I'd done it with Shaun?' Kathryn said.

Kathryn's question took Mackenzie back to that horrible day. She remembered the out-of-the-blue letter sent to her then-workplace. She remembered the request from Paul and Claire Calon, Shaun's parents, for a meeting alone with her at their house and the instruction not to tell Shaun. At that meeting, Claire had remained completely silent. Paul, whilst blushing and trying not to meet her eye, told her what his son had done. When Mackenzie had protested that Shaun wouldn't do that, Paul had asked her where Shaun had been the Thursday before last. All Mackenzie had been able to say was: "Not with me." Shaun hadn't told Mackenzie what he'd done that day, and she hadn't thought to question it. Paul then told her. He revealed Shaun had been at the house of Kathryn Carlisle, having sex with her. Shock had rendered Mackenzie speechless. Taking advantage of Mackenzie's silence, Paul had gone on to explain that, after sleeping with Kathryn, Shaun had gone running to his parents, asking for advice about what to do. The advice Paul said he'd given his son was: "Fess up and tell Mackenzie." When Paul and Claire realised Shaun hadn't done that, they decided that in good conscience, *they* had to do it. That day, sitting on Paul and Claire's white leather sofa, Mackenzie's world fell apart.

'I know you're lying, Kathryn. His parents told me what you two did. How it was lust at first sight when you met at our work's Christmas party. I thought we were friends, Kathy. We used to moan together with Jackie about how unfair it was that, despite having decent degrees, none of us were allowed to do proper architectural work. The least you can do now is tell the truth,' Mackenzie told Kathryn.

Kathryn sighed. 'This is stupid. I *liked* Shaun at the works do, and actually had him round to fit my kitchen a while back, but I didn't sleep with him. I have nothing further to say to you. Goodbye, Mackenzie,' she said.

The call was ended by Kathryn. Mackenzie rested her phone on the arm of her chair and sighed.

All the hurt and anger she'd felt when Shaun had repeatedly denied cheating came flooding back to Mackenzie. It burned through her as if her veins were full of lava.

When Mackenzie's phone buzzed, she was surprised to see a text from Morton. Only after she'd read it did she remember that she wanted to see him to apologise for her behaviour last night. All thoughts about the kiss they'd shared had been forced out by memories of Shaun and his parents.

The text was Morton offering to meet Mackenzie for a walk around Castle Park during his lunch hour. He said the fresh air might do her good. Mackenzie hoped he was right.

Chapter Thirty-six

Mackenzie underestimated how far out of town her grandad's house was, and how hot the weather was. She arrived at the gates of Castle Park ten minutes late, sweating and slightly dizzy. There was no sign of Morton.

When Morton had text Mackenzie, he'd given her an exact location to meet using an app that gave every 3m square in the world a name made up of 3 random words. The app confirmed she was in the agreed square.

Just as Mackenzie was beginning to wonder if Morton had decided not to wait for her, she spotted him running into the park.

'Sorry. Something is up with the clock on my desk, and it took me a while to notice,' Morton told Mackenzie when he got to her.

'I was late too. It's further than I thought, and far too hot for running. My excuse is that I'm hungover,' Mackenzie replied.

'But *I* just ran here from the office. What you mean is, it is too hot for *you* to run. It *isn't* far too hot for running in general,' Morton pointed out.

Mackenzie sighed. 'You are so pedantic,' she told Morton. After the words left her mouth, she worried they might offend him.

When Morton laughed, Mackenzie felt relief wash over her. 'There's nothing wrong with saying things accurately,' he said to her.

Something about Morton's sentence reminded Mackenzie of a character in a sitcom she'd once watched with her mum. An American one, set somewhere like Boston or New York. The character she was thinking of worked as a teacher, as far as she could remember.

'Let's get walking,' Mackenzie said.

Morton and Mackenzie strolled at a steady pace along the tarmacked path. They paused by a bench which Mackenzie had spotted a squirrel on that she wanted to photograph. When Mackenzie got her phone out and the squirrel started advancing towards her, she and Morton swiftly moved on.

After ambling downhill for a few minutes, Morton asked: 'What did you call me here for? Was there something you forgot to tell me last night?'

This was the moment Mackenzie had been waiting for, and dreading. 'It's about me kissing you. I wanted to apologise,' she said.

When she'd imagined apologising to Morton, she'd pictured him stopping to look her in the eye. He did not. They continued plodding along.

'What possessed you to kiss me?' Morton questioned.

As Mackenzie had been asking herself that question since she'd opened her eyes that morning, it was easy to answer Morton. 'Red wine. I have never been drunk. I rarely drink alcohol, and when I do it's beer, which is a lot weaker than wine. Because it was so unfamiliar, and because you'd been so nice to me, I confused the feeling of being drunk with the feeling of being in love. I'm really sorry, Morton. I *don't* love you,' she explained.

While trying to get to sleep the previous night, Morton had

wondered why Mackenzie had kissed him. After concluding it had to be the effects of the wine, he'd drifted off. It pleased him to know he was right. In bed, and with Mackenzie walking past a cafe in the park, Morton had replayed his *first* kiss.

Focusing on the future, Morton said: 'Ah, so if I want a girl to kiss me, I have to either get her drunk or have someone pay her.'

'What do you mean about paying?' Mackenzie questioned.

'My first kiss, which was my *only* kiss prior to last night, was from Daphne Mary Little, the most conventionally attractive girl in school. It was, I have to say, a lot better than last night. Her lips were soft, she was wearing a really gentle floral perfume, and it lasted a few precious seconds. She'd never spoken to me before, and she didn't speak to me when she kissed me either. She just came over, ran her delicate little hand through my hair, and brushed her lips against mine. I did wonder what she was doing, but I was too stunned to question it properly. The next day, I found out that Daphne's best friend had bet her that she couldn't kiss me, "the most unkissable boy in class". Of course, Daphne proved her friend wrong, so she had to give her a fifty-pound voucher to spend in Fenwick's,' Morton explained, imitating Daphne's friend's accent when he quoted her.

When Mackenzie had been at school, she'd hardly been the most popular girl in her class, but there had been a few boys who'd been more than willing to kiss her. Remembering those kisses made her cringe. She couldn't imagine how Morton felt that he'd only been kissed by a girl who was dared to, and a woman who'd been drunk.

So lost in her thoughts was Mackenzie that she hadn't noticed she and Morton had come to a gap in a historic brick wall and were about to cross a cycle path. Thanks to Morton putting a hand out to stop her, she did not get run down by cyclists.

'I'm okay about the fact that Daphne only kissed me because of the bet. As Jude pointed out at the time, I enjoyed the kiss, and wouldn't have wanted anything more from her. It doesn't matter *why* she kissed me,' Morton told Mackenzie.

As they crossed the cycle path, Mackenzie questioned: 'So it doesn't bother you that she kissed you? How about *me* kissing you?'

While he considered how to put his feelings about Mackenzie kissing him into words, Morton noticed a family eating sandwiches while sitting on a plastic-backed blanket laid out on the grass. It reminded him that he had to buy a card for Cecilia, who had celebrated her last birthday with a picnic. It hadn't been necessary to buy her a card that year, for he hadn't really known her.

'*You* kissing me is different to Daphne. I enjoyed Daphne's kiss, but I must admit that I hated yours. That's partly because you stank of the wine that had driven you to do it. Mostly, I'm just worried about you. I take it as a very bad sign of the state you're in that you thought it was a good idea to kiss me,' Morton revealed.

'Oh, Morton! A girl doesn't have to be paid, or drunk, or messed up in the head, to want to kiss you. As for the state I'm in, I felt much better when I woke up this morning, mentally I mean. Physically I was, and still am, *rough*, but I'll get over that. You really helped,' Mackenzie told him.

'Thanks,' Morton mumbled.

Having talked about what they were in the park to discuss, Mackenzie and Morton followed the meandering path downhill in silence. In that silence, they both thought about how nice it was to be with someone who didn't feel the need to talk non-stop all the time.

As soon as she parted ways with Morton and set off home, Mackenzie started thinking about Kathy. They'd been good friends at work, and not once had Kathy mentioned she was gay. She had also never talked about a partner, of any gender.

While walking along the High Street, Mackenzie got her phone out. This forced everyone else walking on the High Street to dodge her.

Paying no attention to her surroundings, Mackenzie opened Facebook and navigated to Kathryn Carlisle's profile. Her profile picture was of her and another woman with a rainbow superimposed on it. When she scrolled down, Mackenzie found photos of Kathryn and the woman in her profile picture at Chatsworth House. That didn't help her, so she kept scrolling.

When she almost tripped up a step, Mackenzie decided it would be best to pull to one side and stop walking so she wasn't at risk of falling or in anyone's way. As soon as she'd paused, Mackenzie spotted what she'd been looking for. A post that read: "So happy to make my relationship with Leigh "Facebook Official". Yes, in case you are wondering, Leigh is a woman, as am I. No, in case you are wondering, I haven't been hiding the fact that I'm a lesbian. I just didn't advertise it. Now I want to share my love for Leigh with the world, I am also sharing my sexuality. If this offends you, then I suggest you take a look at your calendar, which will point out to you that this is the 21st century. Thanks, Kathy."

What she'd just read shocked Mackenzie. It, and the dozens of kind comments on it from Kathy's friends and family, confirmed to Mackenzie that she was definitely gay, and very in love with Leigh. It made her head spin. For the first time since leaving their house, Mackenzie wondered if Shaun's parents had lied.

Chapter Thirty-seven

'Can I put "master photographer" on my CV now?' Mackenzie asked her grandad after photographing ten different lamps, on and off, for Wight's Antiques's website.

Mr Wight laughed. 'No. I didn't ask for them to be blurry. Besides, you don't need to add to your CV. You've got a good work ethic and a degree. What more could an employer want?' he replied.

"What more could an employer want?" was a question Mackenzie had asked herself several times in her previous job. She'd come up with one answer, which she decided to share with her grandad. 'They could want me to be male or older,' Mackenzie suggested.

'That's true of some places, I suppose. Not here though. Here we just want people, male, female, or other, who can take decent photos,' Mr Wight said.

While filling the shop with her laughter, Mackenzie returned to the stockroom so she could attempt to take a decent photo or twenty.

At some point while Mackenzie was taking photos in the stockroom, her uncle came into the shop. She heard Eddie greet her grandad before making his way into the office.

When she'd taken all the required photos and checked that they were decent, Mackenzie went to see her grandad, who was talking to someone at the counter.

'Ah, and here is my granddaughter. Now, she is exactly the sort of person we were talking about. She can do sums in her head that I couldn't do with a calculator, she can draw up complicated but perfect plans to restore old buildings, but can't take a photo to save her life,' Mr Wight told the woman he was speaking to.

'To save her life? How badly do you treat your staff, George?' the customer questioned with a smile on her face.

'Well, you might see, depending on the quality of these pictures,' Mr Wight replied.

When her grandad held out his hand, Mackenzie gave him the digital camera she'd taken pictures with. With a serious expression on his face, Mr Wight flicked through each image and examined them. He even zoomed in on some of them.

While they waited, Mackenzie and the customer exchanged a comically over-the-top nervous look.

As he handed the camera back to her, Mr Wight told his granddaughter: 'They're all good. You get to live another day. Slap them up on the website, please.'

Turning to his customer, Mr Wight said: 'I mean, good work, Mackenzie. You are a valued employee and vital cog in the machine. Your next task is to create engaging and professional virtual adverts for our stock.'

For at least the second time that day, Mackenzie burst out laughing. She said goodbye to her grandad and took herself off to the office.

As she walked away, Mackenzie heard the customer say: 'I'll have the cupboard, please. Soon my floor will be free of Stan's models.'

A few seconds after Mackenzie had sat down in the black spinney office chair covered in scratchy fabric, the phone rang. This would have been irritating for someone not in reach of the phone who was busy. As Mackenzie was sitting right in front of the phone and had no tasks that urgently needed completing, it was no bother to her to remove the handset from the holder and accept the call.

'Good morning, Wight's Antiques. How may we help you?' Mackenzie enquired. The tone of voice she used was one she'd acquired while working for the architectural practice in Sheffield. A manager had complained that customers couldn't understand her Northern accent she'd had at the time, and had given her elocution lessons. At the time, this inspired Mackenzie to talk in as thick an accent as possible when not at work. The memory made her smile.

'Morning. Is Edward Wight there?' the person on the phone to Mackenzie in the present day asked.

The mention of her uncle reminded Mackenzie that she was supposed to be watching him for signs of wrongdoing. It was as if a physical weight rested on her shoulders when it occurred to her that this call could be what revealed Eddie to be a villain.

'I believe he is available. What is this regarding?' Mackenzie asked.

'The details of an order he's placed with us. The account details and billing address are what we'd expect, but not where it is to be delivered. The address he's given appears to be residential, so we wondered if he'd accidentally put his home address instead of work,' the person on the phone explained.

That set alarm bells ringing in Mackenzie's head. The business was paying for an order which was being delivered to Eddie's house.

'One moment, please,' Mackenzie told the person on the phone.

As there was nothing else she could do, Mackenzie took the

handset into the stockroom, in which she saw a couple of tables, a large mirror, ten lamps, plenty of empty space, and Eddie Wight.

'Phone for you. A company asking about the address for an order. It seems you've told them to send it to your house,' Mackenzie told Eddie.

Without blushing, and perfectly able to hold Mackenzie's gaze, Eddie took the phone and said: 'Thanks. That will be my suitcases.'

So Eddie felt like he had privacy, Mackenzie returned to the office. She remained just inside the doorway, where she could hear Eddie confirm an address to the person on the phone. It was his address. He went on to confirm that Wight's Antiques were to be charged for the order.

Mackenzie could imagine what her mum would say if she told her. Dawn Wight would declare her brother-in-law to be a thief, and would go on about how she'd always thought he was a bad sort. As for *Mackenzie* Wight, she wasn't sure what to think.

Instead of thinking, Mackenzie started creating listings on Wight's Antiques's website for the lamps she'd photographed.

—

When Mackenzie had finished adding the lamps to Wight's Antiques's website, she decided to check what the listings looked like on the mobile version of the site. To do this, she got her phone out and typed "Antique lamps Colchester" into a search engine. She knew the exact address of Wight's Antiques's website, so could have gone to it directly. As she was curious to see how far up it was in the results from the search engine, she didn't.

It pleased Mackenzie to see that Wight's Antiques were fifth in the search engine's results. Above them were two online auction sites, which she'd expected, a fellow antique shop in Colchester called Bygones, and an online shop named Colne Valley Upcycling. The picture by the listing for Bygones, which showed the shop front with rails just inside the window full of vintage clothes, looked familiar to her. It also looked enticing. Had she have been looking to go shopping instead of just doing research for work purposes, she'd have headed straight to Bygones and rifled through their rails.

As part of her wondered why a listing for an online shop that she'd never heard of was above Wight's Antiques, Mackenzie clicked on their link. It brought up a page full of in-focus photos of various antique items with light bulbs implanted in them. When her eyes were drawn to a bright red petrol can with three little dents in the front and a bulb sticking out of the top, she rolled her eyes. To her, the lamp lacked any personality, and its modern bulb and perfect paint job hid almost all traces of its history. The only thing she liked was that, because of where they were placed, the three dents made it look like the former petrol can was smiling.

After noticing that the petrol can appeared to be smiling, she remembered that wasn't the first time she'd thought that. It also wasn't the first time she'd seen that petrol can. The first time she'd seen the seemingly-smiling petrol can was in Battlesbridge, where her grandad and uncle had purchased it using the Wight's Antiques business account.

It occurred to Mackenzie that she hadn't seen the petrol can since the day it was purchased. She hadn't seen it in the stockroom or on the shop floor once.

To check she hadn't imagined her grandad and uncle purchasing a petrol can, Mackenzie got the notebook that had a record of everything the business had purchased out of the drawer. As they were in the same drawer, she also removed the inventory and record of what had been sold.

When she flicked back through the notebook to the day she'd been to Battlesbridge, Mackenzie found an entry for "£20 Battlesbridge Antiques Centre – Red vintage petrol can – paint flaking off and three dents in front" written in her handwriting.

The petrol can that had indeed been purchased by Wight's

Antiques in Battlesbridge wasn't in the inventory or the record of sold items. Something didn't add up. Mackenzie groaned when she realised she'd have to work out if someone had forgotten to note that they'd sold it, or if something more sinister had happened.

As Mackenzie ran a hand through her hair in the hope it would help her work out what to do, Eddie walked in and asked: 'Are you okay?'

The sight of her uncle promoted Mackenzie to think: '*Did you steal it to sell on to these upcycling people?*'

38

Chapter Thirty-eight

Hours of looking at screens, and the information she'd read on them, left Mackenzie unable to sleep.

First, Mackenzie had checked every journal roll printed since the trip to Battlesbridge, which listed all the transactions that had gone through the till, against the notebook that listed everything that had been sold. The notebook said exactly what had been sold as well as how much for, whereas the journal roll only had amounts. She was hoping there'd be an amount on the journal roll that wasn't in the notebook. Sadly for Mackenzie, it matched perfectly.

Mackenzie had gone on to wonder if the petrol can had been paid for, but for some reason the money hadn't gone through the till. To check, she used online banking to view a list of all the money paid into the account. She knew that all the takings from each day were paid into the bank on the next day, except on Saturdays. Her grandad didn't like to keep too much cash on the premises. Every amount paid in matched the amount on the Z read from the till printed the day before. There was no extra thirty-five or forty pounds that could have been the petrol can.

Having established that the petrol can definitely hadn't been paid for, Mackenzie came to the conclusion that Eddie had stolen it, and probably a lot of other things. She didn't know how to tell her grandad. There was plenty of proof that it hadn't been paid for, but nothing to say Eddie was the one who'd taken it. Mackenzie herself could just as easily have been the thief. Just because she said Eddie had done wrong, it didn't mean her grandad would believe her. Her grandad and uncle were very close.

'But you believed someone when they told you someone you were close to had done wrong, didn't you Mackenzie? All Shaun's parents had to do to convince you was name the person he'd done wrong with and where they'd met. You assumed that his own family wouldn't lie,' a voice in Mackenzie's head pointed out.

'Well, that's different. I'm Eddie's niece, not his parents, and I'll be the only one accusing him,' Mackenzie silently replied to herself.

The argument in Mackenzie's head paused when she realised something else. 'Only *one* person accused *Shaun*! His mum never spoke a word to me, except "hello"!' she exclaimed out loud.

Right then, laying wide awake in her bed, Mackenzie was almost sure Eddie *was* stealing from her grandad, and she was almost sure Shaun *hadn't* cheated on her. She knew how to confirm that Shaun had done nothing wrong. It would mean going to Sheffield, which put a smile on her face.

39

Chapter Thirty-nine

The moment Mackenzie stepped off the train, calm washed over her. She sauntered up to the barriers and fed her ticket in. When they opened, she skipped through them as if they lead to paradise. To Mackenzie, Sheffield *was* paradise, or as close to it as was possible on Earth.

Outside the station, the sun was beaming, yet the air was refreshing and light. It made walking through the city all the more pleasant. Even if it had been raining, as it often was in Sheffield, Mackenzie would have enjoyed herself. She was strolling through her hometown to make sure that the love of her life hadn't cheated.

As it was roughly between her and her destination, Mackenzie meandered past The Crucible Theatre. Just being in its vicinity filled her with pride in her city for being the home of a truly beautiful game, and gave her a tingle of excitement when she thought about the fact that her sporting heroes would have walked on the same grey bricks as her on the biggest days of their careers.

The many hills she had to go up and down tired Mackenzie and tempered her enthusiasm. She took it as a sign she'd gone soft while Down South. Colchester had a few hills which were considered steep by the locals, but they were nothing compared to the hills around Sheffield.

When she eventually arrived at her destination, Mackenzie was quite glad. As much as she loved walking around her hometown, she could only put up with the burning sensation in her legs for so long.

Just like she had on one of the worst days of her life, Mackenzie knocked the twisted wrought iron door knocker four times.

A few seconds after Mackenzie had knocked on it, Claire Calon opened the door. 'Hel... Oh!' Claire said when she saw who her visitor was.

'There's something I need to ask you,' Mackenzie told Claire, pushing her way past her and into the house.

Even though she could hear Claire protesting behind her, Mackenzie didn't stop until she'd reached the lounge. It had the same white leather sofas in that she'd sat in that day when her happy relationship with Shaun had shattered into a million pieces.

When Claire reached her lounge, she found Mackenzie sat on one of the sofas, arms folded and legs crossed.

'Why did you lie to me?' Mackenzie asked.

Claire spluttered. 'Lie? What are you talking about? Why have you barged into my house? If Paul was here, he'd throw you out, I tell you, and it wouldn't be pretty,' she replied.

That told Mackenzie she'd got Claire to herself, which was exactly what she'd wanted. Claire was the key to the truth.

'You told me your son, the man I adore, had cheated on me. That was a lie,' Mackenzie explained.

Unsure of what to do, Claire sank down onto the sofa opposite Mackenzie. When Mackenzie raised an expectant eyebrow at her, Claire realised she had to say something.

'Lie? Why do you think we lied?' Claire questioned.

There was a slight wobble in Claire's voice. It told Mackenzie she'd been right to travel hundreds of miles to confront her. Claire was about to crack.

'Was it *not* a lie then? Did Shaun really sleep with Kathy Carlisle, a lesbian, when he was in a relationship with me?' Mackenzie replied.

As Mackenzie had expected, Claire didn't answer. That, in itself, was an answer. It was the answer Mackenzie had dreamt of.

'*Why* did you lie?' Mackenzie repeated.

The moment Claire gave in, Mackenzie saw it in her eyes. They began to burn with rage. At last, she was going to get an admission and explanation.

'Shaun could have gone to Oxford or Cambridge. He could have gone on to take a top job in The City. Not *this* pile of crap that *calls* itself a city. I'm talking about The City of London,' Claire began.

Mackenzie shrugged. 'And what does that have to do with me?' she asked.

After jumping out of her seat, Claire ranted: 'It has *everything* to do with you! Shaun is a handsome and smart man who is more than capable of getting himself a pretty, feminine wife and providing for her and the well-behaved little children they'd have together. He was on course to lead a great life, where he was respected and achieved noteworthy things. Then *you* came along. You with your manly job and brash, loud, ways. You who convinced him that he couldn't do better than Sheffield. You who has nothing to show for herself except a piece of paper from what is hardly the finest educational establishment in the country. Just because *you'll* never amount to anything, doesn't mean you had to clip the wings of our Shaun and extinguish his ambition.'

Not once during their relationship had Shaun expressed a wish to study or work anywhere other than Sheffield. One of the first things he and Mackenzie had bonded over was their shared love of their hometown.

Something Shaun hadn't talked about much was his parents. He'd told Mackenzie about his childhood and how his dad had always pushed him to be the best at everything he did, but he'd not discussed what his relationship with them was like as an adult. It hadn't occurred to Mackenzie to question it. Many people drift away from their parents a bit when they become adults.

'Why are you even here? What possessed me to let you in? Get out! Get out of my house!' Claire cried, standing over Mackenzie.

With a smile on her face, Mackenzie sprang to her feet. 'Show me out then,' she replied.

When Claire stormed out of the lounge, into the hall, and pulled the front door open, Mackenzie followed her. The moment she stepped out of Shaun's parent's house and was welcomed by the fresh spring air, she felt a weight lift off her shoulders.

Before sauntering off up the garden path, Mackenzie turned to Claire and told her: 'I came to confirm I was right that Paul lied to me and made you go along with it. Thanks for helping me with that. Now I know Shaun is the good man I originally thought he was, I can get back with him.'

The horror of realising Mackenzie was going to be part of her son's life once again left Claire speechless.

In the few seconds it took her to get from Claire's front door to the pavement, Mackenzie thought of something else she wanted to say to her. 'By the way, should Shaun and I ever have kids, I'll make sure you never see them,' Mackenzie called to her.

In response, Claire slammed the door.

Amused by Claire's anger, Mackenzie made her way to the nearest tram stop with a spring in her step.

Once she'd got on the tram, Mackenzie thought about how

it wasn't just her relationship with Shaun that his parents had destroyed. Because they'd named Kathy Carlisle as Shaun's bit on the side, they'd ruined Mackenzie's relationship with her too.

Thinking of how she'd spoken to Kathy, Mackenzie decided to send her a quick text. "Hi, Kathy. I'm really sorry about accusing you of cheating with Shaun. I know you didn't. I now know no-one did. Please accept this apology and enjoy your trip to London with Leigh" she typed.

Having established for certain that Shaun was innocent, and apologised to Kathy, Mackenzie felt a lot lighter.

On the journey home, Mackenzie started to process that she knew for sure Shaun hadn't cheated, so they hopefully once again had a future together. Part of her was itching to rush over to his house and tell him she knew the truth, but she resisted it. Before telling Shaun, she needed to give herself time to truly believe it. She figured that after talking to her dad about Eddie, listening to her mum drivel on, and a good night's sleep in her own bed, it would sink in.

40

Chapter Forty

When Mackenzie got to her family home, Alf was waiting for her.

'So, Dad told me you missed us, and that's why he'd given you a few days off to come up here. As lovely as that is, something tells me that's not why you're *really* here,' Alf said to Mackenzie after handing her a cup of tea.

Mackenzie had decided not to tell her family that she now knew Shaun hadn't cheated. Britney hated Shaun, and Mackenzie worried that her sister and the rest of the family wouldn't understand why she now wanted him back. Once Mackenzie had gone to Shaun's house and professed her undying love to him, she'd take a selfie with him and send it to all the family with an explanation.

'I have news about uncle Eddie,' Mackenzie told her dad.

It pained Mackenzie to see the disappointment in her dad's face. 'Go on then. What have you found?' Alf asked.

It took Mackenzie a while to tell her dad that she thought Eddie bought things with the Wight's Antiques account, had them delivered to his house, and sold them on to an upcycling company. As Mackenzie had expected, Alf asked if there was proof. After she explained to him how thorough she'd been going through paperwork, and what she'd overheard, lines developed in his forehead.

'Well, well, well, he really *is* up to no good. That *does* surprise me. I thought Ed loved Dad like *I* did. Evidently not,' Alf muttered.

Wanting to make her dad feel better, Mackenzie pointed out: 'Eddie isn't paid. Maybe that's why he's done this. Perhaps he feels it's what he deserves.'

Alf sighed. 'No. If he wanted money, he should have just asked. Dad pays *you*. I'm sure he'd have been happy to pay Eddie,' he replied.

For a while, the only sound in the lounge was that of Mackenzie and her dad sipping tea. She didn't know what to say. It upset *her* that Eddie was a thief. She couldn't imagine how it felt for the man who'd grown up with him.

It wasn't just Mackenzie who was upset and didn't know what to say. Mackenzie's dad couldn't find the words to express his disappointment, and didn't particularly want to share his feelings anyway.

To avoid showing his daughter how hurt he was, Alf decided to change the subject a bit. 'How is my dad?' he asked.

When Mackenzie thought of her grandad, Hazel came to mind. 'He's good, thank you. He was quite happy to let me have time off so I could come up here,' she told her dad.

'And? I sense there's something else,' Alf replied.

The fact that her dad knew she was hiding something warmed Mackenzie's heart. She was well aware of how lucky she was to have such a loving and supportive family that understood her and cared about her. Many people, Shaun included, had to live without the luxury of family love.

It was difficult for Mackenzie to decide whether or not to tell her dad about Hazel. He was already sad. She didn't want to make him anxious too. It would make her feel better though, to tell him, and if she didn't then he'd know she was keeping something from him.

'Our next-door neighbour is getting quite friendly with Grandad. She's had him do up the garden, and the other day he went over to hers to help her set up her new Kindle and stayed for dinner. Her name is Hazel and, as far as I know, she lives alone and is around Grandad's age,' Mackenzie revealed.

Alf smiled. 'Well, that's great! I did worry he'd be lonely forever after Mum left him, but maybe not,' he said.

As that wasn't the response she'd expected, Mackenzie frowned.

'What?' Alf asked.

'Doesn't it worry you that Hazel might have an ulterior motive?' Mackenzie questioned.

'Erm, no. Your grandad is a kind and loveable person. You don't need a hidden agenda to want to spend time with him. *You're obviously concerned though. Is that because of something you've seen, or your own experiences?*' Alf replied.

From the moment she'd met her, Mackenzie had been suspicious of Hazel. Because of this, she'd paid close attention to all Hazel's dealings with her grandad. When she recalled all the little things that she'd noticed, Mackenzie couldn't see any just cause for her suspicion.

'I don't know why I thought so badly of her. Hazel hasn't done anything wrong,' Mackenzie realised aloud.

Alf sighed. '*I know why. Someone betrayed you. Because you didn't see that coming, and you thought he could be trusted, now you question everything*,' he told his daughter.

'You're right, but all that's going to change soon. From now on, I'm going to do my best to have faith in humanity,' Mackenzie declared.

41

Chapter Forty-one

After telling her family that she fancied shopping at Meadowhall, a large shopping centre, Mackenzie made her way across town by foot and tram to Shaun's house. Dreaming of how happy Shaun would be to see her, she rapped her knuckles on his door.

When there was no answer, Mackenzie began to wonder if Shaun was at work. There wasn't a car on the drive. She was so overwhelmed by the excitement of telling him she knew the truth that it hadn't occurred to her he may not be at home.

Just in case Shaun was home and hadn't heard the door, Mackenzie got her phone out and called him. 'This person's phone is currently switched off,' her phone told her.

Instead of throwing her valuable and useful iPhone on the floor, like she wanted to, Mackenzie took a deep breath. All she wanted was to see Shaun, but she hadn't realised how difficult it would be.

If Shaun had a desk job, Mackenzie would march into his office and demand to see him. Unfortunately for her, he didn't. He was a carpenter, and could be anywhere. Part of her was tempted to knock on every door in Sheffield and ask if Shaun was doing work for them, but she knew that wasn't practical.

Suddenly, Mackenzie thought of someone who *might* know where Shaun was. As that someone was on the opposite side of town, Mackenzie set off up the road to get back to the tram stop.

After making her way across town by tram and foot, Mackenzie reached her local corner shop. There, she found Hazeem, who was bent over cleaning up a spillage in one of the narrow aisles with a mop that was too short for him.

'Hazeem! I need to ask you something!' Mackenzie called to him.

When he straightened up and saw Mackenzie, Hazeem frowned. 'You're *here*!' he cried.

It puzzled Mackenzie that Hazeem was so surprised to see her in her family's local shop, but she disregarded her confusion. 'Yes, I'm visiting. Do you know where Shaun is?' Mackenzie asked.

Hazeem pushed his fingers through his thick black hair. 'On the M1, probably,' he told Mackenzie.

Though she'd hoped that Hazeem would say Shaun was in Sheffield, Mackenzie was at least relieved that Hazeem knew where he was. Now all she had to do was be patient and wait until Shaun returned from wherever it was he was off to.

'So he's not in town. That's something. When will he be back home?' Mackenzie replied.

'When he finds you, based on what he told me earlier, but you're here and he's there. It's all gone wrong for him,' Hazeem muttered.

As she was aware how worked up she was, it didn't surprise Mackenzie that what Hazeem was saying didn't make sense to her. What did surprise her was, after she'd taken a few deep breaths and replayed Hazeem's words in her head, they *still* didn't make sense. From what she'd understood of Hazeem's mutterings, *Shaun* was looking for *her*, and was driving somewhere, she assumed

Colchester, to find her. If that was the case, she was in completely the wrong place.

'Hang on, Hazeem. Answer this clearly, please. Is Shaun on his way to Colchester in search of me?' Mackenzie asked, forcing herself to stay calm.

'Yes! Shaun drove to your house, but your mother answered and said you'd moved. Then he came here because he thought I might have a spare phone, but no luck for him. My sister had it off me some time ago. I asked him why he needed a spare, and he told me he was on his way to see you. He said something had obviously changed with you, but I don't know what. In his haste to see you, he didn't put his phone in his pocket properly and it fell out. It wasn't even worth rushing, because you weren't there. Apparently, your mother answered and told him you didn't live there anymore. I remembered you lived Down South in a town with oysters and Romans, but the name escaped me. I suggested he Google "town with oysters and Romans", but of course he couldn't, as he has no phone. He's a clever man though, so he knew I was on about Colchester. As soon as we'd worked it out, he ran out to his car to drive Down South,' Hazeem rambled.

As soon as Hazeem had confirmed Shaun was on his way to Colchester, Mackenzie had wanted to sprint out the door. Out of politeness, she had let him finish. It infuriated her, firstly, that he'd taken so long to answer, secondly, that her family hadn't told Shaun she was in Sheffield, and thirdly, that she and Shaun had probably passed each other while running around town.

When she realised that she did at least now know where to look for Shaun, Mackenzie's fury was replaced by a rush of joy. Yes, Shaun was hundreds of miles from her, but by train she could be with him by teatime, or earlier if she was lucky.

'Thanks, Hazeem. As I'm sure you can understand, I've got to go now,' Mackenzie said.

Full of energy, Mackenzie jogged back home.

42

Chapter Forty-two

When she got through her front door, Mackenzie headed straight upstairs to her bedroom. She didn't want to waste a single second of time that could be spent with Shaun.

Under Mackenzie's bed was her overnight bag, for that is where she'd dumped it the day before. She pulled it out and slung it on the end of the bed.

Just after Mackenzie had got her bag open, ready to throw things into, her door opened and Britney came through it.

'What are you doing?' Britney asked.

'Packing,' Mackenzie replied as she yanked the drawer in her bedside table open and chucked the contents into her bag.

After a hairbrush flew past her nose, Britney decided to take a step back. Mackenzie was her calm and steady older sister. She'd never seen her in such a state. Suddenly, it occurred to Britney what, or rather, *who*, had got her sister so worked up.

'If you've heard that Shaun's been here and are panicking and running away, don't. Mum dealt with him really well. She simply told him you'd moved, and hadn't given permission for the family to tell anyone where you'd gone. It was the most clear and concise speech she's ever given. I doubt he'll bother you ever again. He doesn't even know where you are,' Britney assured her sister.

'No, he *doesn't* know where I am, but I wish he did. I got up at the crack of dawn to go to his house and see him, and now I'm going to have to spend hours on a stuffy train chasing him down the country,' Mackenzie replied.

As Mackenzie had moved hundreds of miles to get away from Shaun, Britney couldn't understand why she'd gone to see him, and why she wanted him to know where she was. Neither Mackenzie's words, nor her actions, made sense.

'Mackenzie, what is going on? Are you well?' Britney asked.

It hadn't occurred to Mackenzie that her behaviour would seem strange to her family. She hadn't even thought about her family, except that she was angry with her mother for lying to Shaun. To reassure her sister, she realised she'd have to explain herself.

'Shaun's parents lied. I found that out for certain yesterday. I still love him, more than ever actually, so I want to tell him that. For a reason I don't know yet, he knows I know the truth and, after finding out from Hazeem that I live there, is on his way to Colchester. I can't call him to tell him I'm not there because he broke his phone this morning in his haste to see me. Had Mum have just told him I was in Sheffield and invited him in for tea, I would not now be throwing my stuff together so I can jump on the first train to London,' Mackenzie explained while zipping her overnight bag up.

'It's not *our* fault! You didn't think to tell us that Shaun's parents lied!' Britney pointed out.

'It was meant to be a surprise!' Mackenzie snapped.

'Well, it definitely is that!' Britney replied.

Both sisters fell silent as they realised what a mess lying had caused. The silence continued as Mackenzie realised how rude she was being.

'Oh, and now I'm snapping at you. As you say, you didn't know any better. Sorry, Brit,' Mackenzie said.

Britney wrapped her sister up in a tight hug. 'Who cares? Shaun didn't cheat. I'm so happy for you,' she replied.

The moment of sisterly affection was broken by Britney shoving Mackenzie off her. 'Now, go find Shaun. Once you've sorted everything out, please thank him for what he did for me,' Britney ordered her sister.

To carry out her sister's orders, Mackenzie kissed her goodbye and set off for the station.

43

Chapter Forty-three

On the train from Sheffield to St Pancras in London, Mackenzie used the search engine on her phone, and a little notebook and pen that she'd bought from the gift shop at Colchester Zoo, to make a list of the phone numbers for every hotel in Colchester. Then, she called each one and asked: 'If you have a guest from Sheffield staying by the name of Shaun Calon, could you tell him that Mackenzie Wight wants to see him?'

After she'd called each hotel, Mackenzie made a note in her book. All of the hotels said that, because of data protection, they could neither confirm nor deny if they had a guest from Sheffield called Shaun Calon staying. A few said they were not the sort of hotel to take messages for guests they already had, let alone *potential* guests. She drew sad faces by the unhelpful hotels. One receptionist assured Mackenzie, if a guest fitting the criteria she'd given checked in, then she'd pass on the message. By that hotel, Bridge House, Mackenzie drew a star.

Once she reached London having had no calls from anyone, it occurred to Mackenzie that Shaun may not check into a hotel. He might get to Colchester, realise he had no way of finding her, and go back home again. That assumed he'd gone to Colchester in the first place.

Like many people, Mackenzie felt thoroughly miserable as she travelled on London Underground.

When she emerged from The Underground at Liverpool Street, Mackenzie's phone buzzed in her pocket several times. As, like most commuters, she wanted to spend as little time at Liverpool Street as possible, she ignored it.

Like every other time Mackenzie had seen it, the concourse at Liverpool Street station was a hive of activity, with swarms of people weaving around each other to get to their respective destinations. She joined the crowds and found her way to a spot where she could look up at the vast electronic information boards that were suspended from the ceiling. Most of the places on the boards, she had never heard of. Based on how many trains went there, she imagined Chingford to be a big and important place.

The first train Mackenzie spotted that stopped at Colchester was a service to Norwich. The only stops on the way between her and Colchester were Stratford and Chelmsford, which pleased her. The fewer places it stopped, the quicker it would be.

Once she'd found her way to platform ten and sat herself down on the train waiting there, Mackenzie got her phone out to check why it had buzzed. When she saw it was notifying her of several missed calls from an 01206 landline, her heart fluttered.

With crossed fingers, Mackenzie tapped to call the Colchester number back. It was answered on the second ring. 'Hello, Bridge House Hotel. How may I help?' a female voice enquired.

'Hi! This is Mackenzie, the girl who left a message for Shaun from Sheffield. You've been calling me, but I didn't get your calls. I was on The Underground,' Mackenzie said.

'Ah, Mackenzie! I'm so glad you called back. I'm Holly, a receptionist at Bridge House Hotel, and I was able to pass that message on to Shaun. He gave me permission to tell you, and thankfully I had the presence of mind to note down your number when you called. He's in front of me now. Do you want to say hello?' the woman on the phone, Holly, asked.

All Mackenzie had wanted since being thrown out by Claire was to speak to Shaun. Now it was possible, she realised she didn't want to have the biggest conversation of her life so far over the phone, with a receptionist and a train carriage full of people listening in.

'No, but thank you, Holly. Thank you so much! You have no idea how much this means to me. Just let him know I'm on a train that's about to leave London. I'll be with him soon,' Mackenzie told Holly.

On Holly's side of the line, Mackenzie could hear her repeating the message.

'Done, and you're welcome. He says he can't wait to see you, and will meet you at the station,' Holly replied.

'You're a star, Holly. I can't thank you enough. Goodbye now,' Mackenzie said.

After Holly had wished her a lovely day, Mackenzie hung up. Partly thanks to Holly, it *was* going to be a lovely day.

Silent tears of relief rolled down Mackenzie's cheeks. A few of her fellow passengers noticed and frowned. None of them asked her if she was okay.

As she was just over an hour away from seeing Shaun, Mackenzie was more than okay.

44

Chapter Forty-four

As her train pulled into Colchester station, Mackenzie was standing by the doors, bag in hand. When the doors opened, she was the first to burst out of them. Her footsteps echoed off the hard surfaces of the station as Mackenzie ran up the platform to the exit.

When she escaped the confines of the station, Mackenzie expected to see Shaun waiting for her just outside the doors. He was nowhere to be seen.

'Shaun?!' Mackenzie called out.

A few people passing by looked over at Mackenzie, but none of them were Shaun.

As she looked around herself once again for Shaun, Mackenzie realised her surroundings were unfamiliar. She'd come out of a different exit to the one she usually used. Instead of a taxi rank in front of her, there was the entrance to a car park.

Relief washed over her as she laughed out loud. She'd been panicking that she would never find Shaun, when he was just the other side of the tracks.

To get to where she was sure Shaun was waiting for her, Mackenzie set off on the five-minute journey to the opposite side of the station. She had to go downhill to get under the bridge that the tracks ran over, along a busy road full of cars waiting to join a roundabout, and then back uphill to the entrance by the taxi rank. She barely noticed the fumes or her tired legs struggling with the umpteenth incline they'd had to take her up that day. All she could think about was the fact that Shaun was waiting for her just a few feet away.

When Mackenzie got to the top of the hill that led to the entrance by the taxi rank, her footsteps slowed. She could see taxis, a man in a suit wheeling a small suitcase, and pigeons, but not Shaun.

'You have got to be kidding me,' Mackenzie muttered to herself.

To confirm her suspicions that Shaun wasn't at Colchester station, Mackenzie went inside the building. Only staff were in there.

As she made her way back out into the spring sunshine, Mackenzie questioned if she'd heard Holly right that Shaun would wait for her at the station. To check that she wasn't going mad, she called Bridge House Hotel for the third time that day.

The second her call was answered, Mackenzie asked: 'Did you say Shaun would meet me at the station?'

'Hello again, Mackenzie. Yes, I did, and he left as soon as you hung up,' Holly confirmed.

That wasn't the answer Mackenzie wanted to hear. She'd hoped that Shaun had stayed at the hotel. Then she'd be able to find him.

'Where are you now?' Holly asked.

'The station, and he's not here!' Mackenzie cried.

'Hang on a moment. Calm down. *Which* station are you at?' Holly questioned.

That question puzzled Mackenzie. As she was already agitated, her confusion manifested as anger. 'Colchester! Where did you think I was, Timbuktu(?!)' she shouted down the phone.

'Calm down, Mackenzie. Please listen to me. Colchester has *two* stations. I'm guessing you're at the north one, as you've come from London. Shaun might have gone to Colchester *Town*,' Holly revealed.

After she'd spoken, it occurred to Holly that Colchester actually had *three* stations, as there was one in the Hythe area. As Hythe was far out of town, she thought it unlikely that Shaun had gone there, so she didn't correct herself.

After she'd spoken, it occurred to Mackenzie that Holly had gone above and beyond to help, and she was being rude to her. She took a few breaths to calm herself down. No-one, let alone someone as lovely as Holly, deserved to be spoken to in the way Mackenzie just had.

'I'm so sorry, Holly. You've been great. Please forgive me for speaking to you like that,' Mackenzie said.

'I understand. Your emotions must be all over the place. Now, stop talking to me, nicely or otherwise, and get yourself over to Colchester Town,' Holly replied.

Looking at the taxis in the rank, Mackenzie decided to do just that. 'Will do. Thanks again for all your help. I've walked all the way across Sheffield today, so I'm not walking across Colchester too. I'll treat myself to a cab,' she told Holly.

'A cab? Is there something wrong with the trains then?' Holly questioned.

When she realised her mistake, Mackenzie roared with laughter. 'Oh, of course I don't need a taxi! I'm at a train station and want to go to *another* train station! How silly am I?' she cried.

On the other end of the phone, Holly laughed too, though not as loudly as Mackenzie had. 'It's okay. Love does this to us all. When someone told me my now-boyfriend had a crush on me, I laughed. I thought it was a joke. Anyway, I won't keep you any longer. I wish you and Shaun the best of luck,' Holly replied.

After saying goodbye to Holly and thanking her again, Mackenzie ended her call and headed back into Colchester station. To avoid accidentally going back to London, which seemed entirely possible considering the day she was having, Mackenzie asked a member of staff to direct her to a train to Colchester Town.

As soon as Mackenzie got out of Colchester Town station, she spotted Shaun, who was checking his watch. Overcome by love, she rushed up to him and threw her arms around him.

Holding Shaun close, all Mackenzie could think about was how nicely her head sat on his chest, as it always had done in the past. They were right by a roundabout full of traffic, but all she could smell was his sweet aftershave, and all she could hear was his heartbeat and breathing. It was a comfortable spring day, but the heat that rushed through her in response to having Shaun's familiar body in her arms made it feel like the height of summer to Mackenzie.

Having held Shaun for several seconds, it occurred to Mackenzie that, knowing her luck, she was embracing a stranger who looked like Shaun at a glance. When she pulled back a little and gazed up, Mackenzie saw a smiling face that was unmistakably Shaun's.

'Hello to you too, Mackenzie,' Shaun said.

With a smile that matched Shaun's, Mackenzie closed her eyes and placed her lips on his. A horn blaring on the roundabout behind Shaun startled Mackenzie and caused her to end their kiss almost as soon as it had begun, but not before she felt him respond and kiss her back.

Though she felt her kiss had said all that needed to be communicated, Mackenzie spoke one word. The one word Mackenzie said was: 'Hi.'

Chapter Forty-five

'As great as it is to be in your arms again, we have a lot of catching up to do, and this isn't the place to do it,' Shaun pointed out.

As she let Shaun go and took in her surroundings, Mackenzie realised that he was right. They couldn't just talk outside Colchester Town railway station, or *any* railway station for that matter.

'They like putting big roundabouts by stations around here,' Mackenzie commented.

'Pardon? I don't get it,' Shaun said.

Mackenzie shook her head. 'Never mind,' she replied.

Commuters bustled past Shaun and Mackenzie, but they were only aware of each other.

'So, do you know any good places to sit and rebuild a relationship around here?' Shaun asked.

For their chat, Mackenzie felt that they needed somewhere private and peaceful. There was nowhere she knew of in Colchester that felt special enough to host such an important conversation. When she thought of places *near* Colchester, she recalled her mum asking her to pick up a painting in St Lawrence, which hadn't been as close as she'd said. That lead Mackenzie to think of somewhere near St Lawrence that was private, peaceful, and the perfect place to sit and rebuild a relationship.

'I know somewhere, but it's not in town,' Mackenzie told Shaun.

'Fine by me. I brought my Jag,' Shaun replied.

Mackenzie gasped. She knew what that meant to Shaun. To check she was right, Mackenzie asked: 'Is it *the one*? The E thing you always wanted?'

'Yes, it is. It was a wreck, and had come from Europe so the steering wheel was on the wrong side, but it was an E-Type that I could afford. Fixing it up kept my mind off you. Now, it's my pride and joy,' Shaun confirmed.

'Oh, congratulations! I'm so happy for you. Please take me to see it,' Mackenzie said.

Holding out his hand to her, Shaun replied: 'I will, if you'll take my hand.'

'We were never the sort of couple who held hands,' Mackenzie pointed out.

'We weren't the sort of couple to hug and kiss by train stations either. Things have changed. Hopefully now, for the better,' Shaun said.

As she thought Shaun had a good point, Mackenzie let him have her hand. It felt so soft and delicate in his, especially when he closed his fingers around hers.

—

Colchester had always seemed soulless to Mackenzie. The architecture showed that much of the town had stood for hundreds of years, but she couldn't feel the history. Walking along its Lanes with Shaun, it felt like a different place. She noticed tourists admiring the sights, and could picture hundreds of them flocking to see the same buildings back in the Victorian era when the railway had arrived. She saw the people walking out of the boutiques with smiles on their faces, and wondered how many generations the little family-run shops had been passed down through.

'So, what do we talk about until we get to this place? This suddenly seems a bit weird. Wonderful, but strange. I don't know what to do with myself,' Shaun said.

'I feel that way too! I'm so glad it's not just me,' Mackenzie replied.

After crossing some roads and giving it some thought, Shaun knew what they could talk about.

'How did you end up here? Do you like it?' he asked.

'I left Sheffield because everywhere I looked, I could picture you. Also, people kept hassling me about the lottery win, asking for money or telling me what to spend it on. I had to get away and have a fresh start. I ended up in Colchester because I have family here. I'm living with my grandad on the outskirts of town, and my uncle is in one of the nearby villages. My grandmother dumped Grandad a couple of years ago, and the family worried he might be lonely,' Mackenzie told Shaun.

'I remember you telling me they'd split, and I think I knew he lived down here. The whole family were shocked. *Is* he lonely?' Shaun replied.

'I think he was, but not so much now. His next-door neighbour has gotten quite friendly with him,' Mackenzie said.

That pleased Shaun. He knew how much Mackenzie loved her family, and he assumed her grandad deserved that love.

Once they saw Bridge House Hotel was in front of them, neither Shaun nor Mackenzie said anything more.

Shaun led Mackenzie around to the back of the hotel, where his green Jaguar E-Type was waiting. When her eyes fell on the car, she let out a little sigh. 'She's so *elegant*! Classic and classy British design. Well done you, for restoring her to her former glory,' she said.

'I'm amused that you've given the car a gender and decided it's female,' Shaun told Mackenzie.

Stroking her hand along the smooth bonnet, Mackenzie said: 'Look at these curves! She's definitely a girl.'

As he opened his door, Shaun chuckled. 'If you say so,' he replied.

After Mackenzie was settled in her seat and had clipped her seatbelt on, Shaun turned the key. The engine purred into life.

'To wherever it is you're thinking of!' Shaun declared as he guided his apparently-female Jag out of the car park and onto the open road.

46

Chapter Forty-six

On the way out of Colchester, Mackenzie only spoke to give directions. Once they were on the road that led past the zoo and down to Tiptree, Mackenzie told Shaun there wouldn't be anything to do for a while.

As her mind wandered, Mackenzie thought about how strange it was that, many times over the last few months, she'd longed to talk to Shaun, yet now she was with him, she didn't know what to say.

It occurred to Mackenzie that, as part of their big conversation, Shaun might ask if she wanted to return to Sheffield with him. There was no doubt in her mind that she wished to go back to Sheffield, but there were things she'd like to do in Colchester first. Her heart sank a little as she remembered, as well as the things she wanted to do, there was something depressing that she *had* to do before leaving Colchester.

The one positive about the thing she had to do was that she could talk to Shaun about it on the drive. 'When we were a couple, we'd share all our problems. Even if the other person didn't have a solution, it helped to discuss them. As we're getting back together, can I tell you about a situation with my uncle and the family business?' Mackenzie asked.

Inside, Shaun cheered when Mackenzie said they were getting back together. He'd suspected as much for a day, but it was great to hear it confirmed.

'Special girl, you can tell me anything,' Shaun told Mackenzie.

Being called "special girl" brought back so many memories for Mackenzie. Other men called their partners "sweetheart" or "darling", but Shaun had never used those words for Mackenzie. Most of the time, he'd used her name. When he did use a pet name, it was always "special girl". As she didn't think that "sweetheart" and "darling" suited her, but liked the idea of being a "special girl", she'd loved it. It told her Shaun knew her inside out.

—

Whilst Shaun raced past a forest and crawled through some roadworks in Tiptree, Mackenzie told him about what her mum had asked her to do, and what she'd found.

'That's tough, especially with a family as tight as yours. It won't be easy for your grandad to hear. Still, it has to be done, and you'll do it just fine,' Shaun commented when Mackenzie was finished.

'But how do I not upset him? I love Grandad, and he's really close to Eddie,' Mackenzie asked.

Shaun puffed his cheeks out. 'I'm sorry to say this, but I don't think you *can* avoid upsetting him. You can minimise it by keeping the emotion out of it, just speaking the facts, and not waffling on,' he replied.

Though she'd already known she couldn't avoid upsetting her grandad, Mackenzie had hoped that Shaun would find a way. She couldn't help but picture her grandad's hurt face when he found out his son was stealing from him, quite possibly in collusion with his estranged ex-wife. The thought made her slump in her seat.

'All you can do is be concise and factual. Basically, don't be your mother,' Shaun told Mackenzie.

It delighted Shaun that his comment made Mackenzie roar with laughter. It hadn't escaped his notice that she was sad, and he'd hoped to cheer her up a bit.

'Oh, how I've missed your laugh,' Shaun said.

'And how *I've* missed your humour,' Mackenzie replied.

Pleased with the compliments they'd given and been given, Mackenzie and Shaun travelled in silence for a while, broken every now and again by directions from Mackenzie.

At some point after going around a fairly large town Shaun didn't notice the name of that had lots of roundabouts (none of which had a railway station by them), a Tesco, and a Morrison's, he wondered why Mackenzie had been to London earlier that day.

'That nice hotel clerk told me you were on a train from London. What were you doing there?' Shaun asked.

Thinking of the story she was about to tell made Mackenzie smile. 'I didn't exactly go *to* London. I passed through it as I dashed back from Sheffield,' she told Shaun.

'Sheffield?! You were there today?! But I called at your house and was told you'd moved. They never said you were there,' Shaun questioned.

'That's because my family don't know yet that you *didn't* cheat on me. At least, they didn't know when you knocked. I told Brit when I was packing, so the whole world probably knows now. Mum lied because she thought she was protecting me. I wasn't home because I was looking for you. I knocked on your door, but *you* weren't home, so I traipsed across town to my local corner shop and asked Hazeem where you were. That's when I found out you were on your way Down South. We must have missed each other by an hour, if that,' Mackenzie revealed.

Shaun shook his head. 'That's crazy,' he muttered.

'Talking about Brit reminds me that she wanted me to thank you for looking after her when she got very drunk. It was really kind of you, especially considering that she's the sister of someone you were mad at. As for today being crazy, there's so much more to the story than I've told you,' Mackenzie replied.

As Shaun didn't know *how* crazy her day had been, and she knew it would amuse him, Mackenzie told him all about calling all the hotels in Colchester, ending up at the wrong station, almost getting a taxi from one station to the other, and panicking about accidentally getting a train to London instead of Colchester Town.

By the time Mackenzie finished recounting her day to Shaun, they were in Bradwell Waterside. She stopped talking so she could hear Shaun's reaction when he realised the road ended in a slipway to the river.

None the wiser, Shaun drove merrily along around a corner and up a slight hill in a small village. When he came to the top of the hill and looked down, he gasped.

'The road becomes a river!' Shaun realised out loud.

'Sort of, yes. I suggest you pull us up on the left somewhere, unless you want to get your beautiful car wet,' Mackenzie said.

'My beautiful, *female* car?' Shaun questioned whilst getting as close to the kerb as he dared.

At the memory of Mackenzie stroking the car and calling it a girl, both she and Shaun laughed.

Chapter Forty-seven

It was to be one of the most important conversations of her life, but Mackenzie didn't know how to start it. Did she just blurt out to Shaun that she'd confronted his mother and got the truth out of her? Did she tell him about Kathy's call to ask where the best places to eat in London were, which was what had first made her suspicious of his parents? There were so many options.

Eventually, Mackenzie decided to kick off by asking Shaun a question. She asked him: 'When did you find out I knew the truth?'

'Last night. I got a message from Kathy saying she was glad you and I had sorted out our issues and good luck to us. This made no sense to me, so I asked her what on Earth she was going on about. In response, she sent a screenshot of a text from you that said you knew I hadn't cheated with anyone. I got so excited then. I had to check with Kathy several times that I'd read it right and you'd really said that. She must have thought I was mad,' Shaun revealed.

Mackenzie bit her lip. That meant Shaun still didn't know it was his parents who had told her he'd cheated. The thought that *she'd* have to tell him what his parents had done made her sick.

'So, now you can tell me what made you think I'd cheated,' Shaun said.

'Remember earlier we were talking about how upsetting it is to have to tell one family member that another has done something wrong?' Mackenzie asked.

When Shaun nodded, Mackenzie knew she had to continue. There was no way of softening it, so she simply blurted out: 'Your parents told me you'd cheated. They sent a letter to my work asking me to come over without telling you, they sat me down on their awful sofas, and your father told me you'd fallen for Kathy at my works do and regularly snuck off to her house to sleep with her.'

It didn't surprise Mackenzie at all that Shaun's response was to swear. The single bad word was followed by silence.

'I knew they weren't impressed by what I told them about you, but I never thought they'd do something like that,' Shaun muttered.

'Why did you never tell me what they were like? I spoke about my family, but you didn't say much about yours. Had I have known how pushy and snobbish they are, I might have seen through their lies. As it was, I had no reason to question them. What sort of father would make up lies like that about his own son?' Mackenzie questioned.

'I worried you'd think me heartless. Your mother drives you mad, but you love her. You adore your family, and the feeling is mutual. They're proud of you no matter what. How can someone from a home like yours understand my upbringing? There have been times when I've hated my father. If I'd have told you that, would you have understood? He didn't beat me up, he just refused to understand me and tried to make me something I'm not, and yet I despise him. What kind of man does that make me?' Shaun replied.

Having once-upon-a-time been as close to him as it was possible to be to someone, Mackenzie knew exactly what sort of man Shaun was. 'You're a caring and passionate man, who knows his own mind. I just wish you'd told me about your family,' she told him.

'Yes, sorry. That was a mistake. As it turns out, that was a *big* mistake. I think it's a lesson to never keep anything from you,' Shaun admitted.

As Mackenzie already thought Shaun shouldn't keep anything from her, she didn't answer. She gave her attention to a seagull, which was gliding over the river.

Something about her surroundings calmed Mackenzie. The peace around her seemed to penetrate her.

'So, you believed my parents for ages, but now you don't. What changed?' Shaun asked.

'I found out that Kathy, who you, a man, apparently slept with, is gay. When I found out that, it made me question everything. It then occurred to me that, when I'd gone to your parents house to see them, only Paul had spoken. I wondered, if Claire was alone, would she admit they'd lied? Anyway, I rushed up to Sheffield, headed straight to your parents house, forced my way in when Claire opened the door and I realised she was alone, and went on at her until she cracked. It seems I, and Sheffield, are not good enough for you. You were destined for an Oxbridge education and a fancy job in finance, and I "clipped your wings" and convinced you to stay Up North and work in carpentry,' Mackenzie revealed, using her fingers for quotation marks.

Shaun tutted. 'Yeah, that's my parents. They could never understand that I wanted to use maths to work out what the best angle was to stick two bits of wood together, not to mess about with other peoples' money. Sounds like you got the measure of my mother. She's your typical Northern woman and doesn't beat around the bush, mince her words, or hide anything. Mum just says exactly what she means. Pops, on the other hand, is sneaky. He tries to manipulate people into doing what he wants. Lying to you will have driven Mum mad, which is probably why she couldn't even speak when you first saw her. I'm glad you know the truth now, not just because it means we can get back together, but because it'll be a weight off Mum's shoulders,' he replied.

It interested Mackenzie that, despite her pressuring him and ruining his relationship, Shaun seemed to care about his mother. It gave her hope that her family would still be able to love Eddie after she exposed him as a thief.

Thinking about Eddie led Mackenzie to wonder, apart from telling her grandad about him, what had to be done before she returned to Sheffield. There was nothing else she could think of that *had* to be done, but there was something she *wanted* to do.

'Can you spend tomorrow down here and we can go home the day after? I'd love you to meet the friends I made here,' Mackenzie asked.

'I've moved the few jobs I had planned for this week, and I can't liaise with clients and plan stuff with them until I replace my phone. I'd *love* to meet your friends,' Shaun replied.

When he thought about being back up in Sheffield with Mackenzie, Shaun wondered something. 'Will you get a job once we're back home? I'm guessing you've still got some of your lottery money, but it won't last. Besides, knowing you I can't imagine you could bear just sitting around all day,' he asked.

Contemplating working made Mackenzie sigh. 'I've barely spent any of my winnings, all I got really was a Parris snooker cue, so it's pretty much all in the bank. I'll be able to put towards your rent without even noticing. You're right though, that for my own good I need a job. I just hope it's better than my last. I want to save and restore precious historical buildings, not make tea for people designing new ones that have no heart, but will make loads of profit,' she said.

Pink and orange stripes in the sky drew Shaun's gaze to the left as an idea formed in his head. Admiring the sunset didn't stop him questioning himself to ensure his plan worked before he presented it to Mackenzie.

'Do you *want* to live in my little house with its single glazed windows and useless heaters? I'm happy to live anywhere you want to. If it was in Yorkshire, I'd be *very* happy. What is your dream house?' Shaun questioned.

When she thought about how she and Shaun had kept warm in his freezing, but cheap, house, Mackenzie felt as hot as she had on those nights. She looked to the right and saw Shaun smiling. He must know what was on her mind, and that made her blush.

Very adult memories were forced out by childhood ones when Mackenzie recalled the crayon drawings she'd made of her dream house. A house she'd gone on to sketch a proper floorplan and architectural drawings for. 'My dream house is a little former workshop or agricultural building, preferably made of limestone, that I can turn into a modern home. When I'd finished with it, it would look as if it had been lived in since the day it was built. It would be in Sheffield, for sure. I long to be back there,' Mackenzie told Shaun.

'With the money you have in the bank, I'm sure you could buy a little old place and have it done up. If you wanted to, you could then set up your own practice or whatever you call it, and use your own home as proof that you know what you're doing,' Shaun pointed out.

'That sounds great! I want to do that. That's my dream, to go back to Sheffield, find a place to turn into a home, work for myself, and live with you in my house for the rest of our lives,' Mackenzie declared.

The enthusiasm with which Mackenzie spoke about their future warmed Shaun's heart. Smiling at her, he said: 'Special girl, if that's your dream, then that's my dream too.'

For a few moments, Mackenzie and Shaun gazed into each others eyes with beaming smiles on their faces. To each of them, it felt as if they were saying "I love you" over and over again.

The romantic moment ended abruptly when Shaun's tummy rumbled so loudly that he and Mackenzie stared at it in wonder. Mackenzie laughed. 'Sounds like we need to drive back and get you some food,' she commented.

'Erm, yes, if that's okay. Sorry to ruin the romantic atmosphere,' Shaun replied.

Mackenzie shook her head. 'Don't worry about it. For me, romance isn't all about getting lost in each others eyes and using pet names for each other. Romance is having someone to lean on. It is having someone's back, and knowing they have yours too. Romance is sharing your life with someone who brings out the best in you, and every situation you find yourselves in. Being hungry can't ruin that, unless you stay hungry for weeks and starve to death,' she told Shaun.

With Mackenzie's definition of romance ringing in his ears, Shaun drove off into the sunset with her.

48

Chapter Forty-eight

The first thing Mackenzie was aware of when she woke up was how warm she was. Next, she noticed the softness of the bedding she was snuggled up under. When she opened her eyes, she saw Shaun smiling back at her.

'Morning, special girl,' Shaun said.

In her dreams, Mackenzie had been running across train tracks, trying to get to Shaun, who was on the other side. A freight train had thundered down the line between them, obscuring her view of him. When the train had passed, and Mackenzie could see all the way across the tracks again, Shaun wasn't there.

Delighted by the discovery that, in real life, Shaun was right next to her, Mackenzie pulled him towards her and held his body tight against hers, settling her head on his smooth chest.

'You're here. Everything is right with the world… Well, *my* world,' Mackenzie mumbled.

Shaun chuckled, which made his chest convulse under Mackenzie's head. 'You're so sweet and uninhibited when you first wake up,' he told her.

'You make a bad pillow when you laugh,' Mackenzie replied.

Despite it being uncomfortable when Shaun laughed, Mackenzie continued to use his chest as a pillow for ten minutes whilst waiting to feel more awake. As she laid there, mundane and random thoughts that had nothing to do with finally sharing a bed with the man she loved after being separate from him for months gradually infiltrated her mind. One of them, which she couldn't help but focus on, convinced her to push herself off Shaun and drag herself out of bed.

'What's up?' Shaun asked.

'I have to shower, throw some clothes on, and get over to Grandad's. The sooner I tell him about Eddie, the sooner I can stop thinking about it,' Mackenzie replied.

As he watched Mackenzie shuffle to the en-suite, Shaun was struck by an urge to call her back to the bed. He wanted her closer and naked, not dressed and on the other side of town. Having just got her back, he knew it would be agonising to watch her walk out the door.

As her hand settled on the handle of the en-suite door, it occurred to Mackenzie that Shaun hadn't answered her. She looked back over her shoulder at him.

'Just remember that you're doing the right thing, and afterwards you can introduce me to your friends. Your family are so lucky to have you, Mackenzie,' Shaun told her.

The encouragement Shaun gave her was exactly what Mackenzie wanted. She smiled and stepped through the door to the bathroom.

After she stepped out of the shower, Mackenzie dried off and got dressed as quickly as possible, in order to reduce the chance of her changing her mind. She had wondered what the moment before she stepped out the hotel room door would be like. Neither she nor Shaun wanted to part, but they knew they had to. When that moment came, Shaun gave Mackenzie a little peck on the forehead and then opened the door for her. Combined with the look in his eyes, it sent a clear message. He loved her, and having to part hurt him just as much as it hurt her, but he supported and understood the thing she was leaving him to do.

On the walk from Bridge House Hotel to her Grandad's house, Mackenzie felt like Shaun was taking every step with her. His love and support was with her even when he wasn't. She hadn't realised how much she'd missed that. Being without it had made life so much harder than it needed to be.

When she got to her Grandad's house, Mackenzie let herself in.

'I'm up in the office. I'll be down in just a moment,' Mr Wight called down the stairs.

As Mackenzie had called Mr Wight from Shaun's hotel room the night before, he was expecting her. She hadn't told him where she was or who she was with. All she'd said was that she'd be back at his house in the morning. All he'd said was that he'd work from home so would see her when she got back. She imagined he'd assumed she was in Sheffield with her family when she'd called.

After less than a minute, Mr Wight made his way down the stairs and into the lounge, where his granddaughter was waiting for him.

'Good to see you back. I hope the trains were okay,' Mr Wight said as he plonked himself down in his winged armchair.

As she saw no need at this stage to tell her grandad she'd been on the train a day ago, not that morning, Mackenzie simply said: 'Yes, they were great, thanks. I got a fast train from London to Colchester.'

Mr Wight nodded. 'That's good. I hope the family are all okay. I'm sure they were delighted to see you,' he replied.

'They're all happy and well. It was worth the journey just for Dad's breakfast,' Mackenzie told her grandad.

Though he didn't react with words, Mackenzie noticed her grandad's attention drift, as if the mention of the breakfast Alf, her dad, his son, made, had reminded him of something.

Unbeknownst to Mackenzie, thinking about his son's breakfast *had* reminded Mr Wight of something. It brought back a memory from when Alf had been a teenager and his then-wife had taught him and Eddie how to fry bacon. Remembering what a wonderful mum his ex-wife had been made him smile. The way their marriage had ended didn't change the fact that she'd been the best parent to their boys that he could have wished for.

Mackenzie took the silence as an opportunity to open the conversation she'd gone there to have. 'Grandad, I need to tell you something. It's not easy, and you might not believe me, but please listen. I promise you I'm telling the truth,' she said.

The tone of voice his granddaughter used brought Mr Wight back to the present. 'Oh? And what's that? Are Alf and Dawn having problems? Was there some kind of row while you were up there?' he asked.

'No, it's not about them. It's about Eddie. This concerns Eddie and your business,' Mackenzie replied.

When she saw the concern and confusion on her grandad's face, Mackenzie realised she needed to get this done with as soon as possible. Otherwise, he'd dream up all kinds of horrible scenarios that were worse than what was actually happening.

Before her grandad could ask her again what was going on, Mackenzie blurted out: 'He's stealing from you. Eddie is buying things with money from the business and selling them on to an upcycling company. I know Wight's Antiques definitely paid for these things he took, and he's not giving the business any money for them. I have scoured notebooks, the things from the till, documents, and even transactions on the bank account to be sure. I'm so sorry, but Eddie is a thief.'

At first, Mackenzie's grandad just stared blankly at her. It made her wonder if he'd actually heard her words. Then, he shook his head. That suggested to her that he *had* heard, but didn't believe her.

'No, Mackenzie, he isn't stealing. My Eddie is not a thief. You've got yourself confused, bless you,' Mr Wight said.

It was just as Mackenzie had feared. Her grandad couldn't accept that his son was stealing from him.

'I really am sorry, Grandad, but I know Eddie is taking things the business owns without paying for them,' Mackenzie told him.

'Yes, he *is* doing that. He has been for a couple of years or so. I know that. I'm just saying he isn't a thief,' Mr Wight replied.

Ever since she'd confirmed Eddie was taking things without paying for them, Mackenzie had dreamt and daydreamt about the moment she had to tell her grandad. On none of those occasions had she imagined that he knew what Eddie was up to.

'What? You know?' Mackenzie questioned.

'Yes. I told him to do it,' Mr Wight revealed.

'Why would you tell your son, or anyone, to steal stuff from your business to sell on?' Mackenzie asked.

'Eddie doesn't sell the items he gets through the shop to an upcycling business. What he does is take them for *his* upcycling business. When I realised that, if I gave him money, he'd spend it on old treasures that he could ruin and then fleece someone into paying fortunes for, I just decided to pay him in stuff. I've been in this trade for decades, and am mates with some of the dealers, so I can get stuff a lot cheaper than Eddie could. It probably goes against some tax law, but it just made sense to me. Personally, I don't get this whole thing of sticking bulbs in just about anything to make fancy lamps, or sanding down a nice oak sideboard that you can see has been loved for generations and spray painting it neon green, but he loves it. I never thought someone would get the wrong end of the stick and accuse him of stealing,' Mr Wight explained.

Now Mackenzie was the one staring blankly at her grandad. The only time she'd felt more stupid was when she'd thought Shaun had cheated on her and she somehow hadn't noticed. The only explanation she'd thought of for Eddie taking stuff was that he was stealing it. She'd never even considered if there could be another, legitimate reason, for him to take the items.

As he sat there in silence, Mr Wight realised that something must have caused his granddaughter to think Eddie was a thief. She hadn't by chance realised that items were being bought but not sold in the shop and jumped to the conclusion that her uncle was stealing them. He had a feeling he knew who it was that had made Mackenzie suspicious.

'The whole thing about thinking Eddie was up to no good. Was it something to do with your parents? Alf was concerned a while back about the fact that Eddie goes to see his mother a lot. I heard them rowing about it on the phone one day. Alf seems to think he has to pick sides, and in order to be in my good books he has to cut ties with his mother just because she left me. Eddie, however, knows that I don't care if you see me *and* her every week if that's what you want. My guess is that Alf told Dawn about how odd he thinks it is that Eddie is close to their mother, and then he also happened to mention that Eddie is helping me with the business. Your mother always has had a wild imagination. I'm sorry to say it, but she is the type to put two and two together and get five-hundred. She absolutely would get suspicious and ask you to check things out. Of course, if you've been told that Eddie's up to no good, you *would* think he's a thief when you found what you found,' Mr Wight questioned.

Mackenzie blushed. 'That's exactly it. Mum got me back up to Sheffield by buying a painting that was down here and listed collection only. Then, she told me she thought Eddie was up to no good and asked me to get involved with the business and look for clues. I'm sorry, Grandad,' she replied.

Mr Wight sighed. 'I can see how it looked to them, and you were all just looking out for me. I should be pleased that you all care about me so much, I suppose,' he said.

The tone of Mr Wight's voice did not suggest that he was pleased. This made Mackenzie hesitant to say anything. As he hardly ever got angry, she didn't know how to handle him when he was cross.

The sound of the doorbell cut loud and clear through the silence in the lounge. Mr Wight eased himself out of his chair and made his way across the room to get to the hall and answer the front door. When he opened it, Hazel was there, clutching her Kindle.

'I've finished it! The twists and turns were *incredible*! Thank you so much for recommending it, and for setting this contraption up so I could enjoy it!' Hazel cried.

'Oh, I *am* pleased that you enjoyed it. What did you think to that bit by the river?' Mr Wight asked.

Hazel shivered. 'That Mr Bellasis is a nasty piece of work. I'm so glad Oliver doesn't listen to him. I didn't like Oliver at first, but he turned out good in the end. Thank goodness, because I thought Charles Pope was sweet. I'd have hated for him to die, especially in such an awful way,' she replied.

The way Hazel spoke about the characters made Mr Wight feel something he hadn't felt in a while. 'I don't know about Charles Pope, but *you're* definitely sweet,' Mr Wight murmured to himself.

As she heard Mr Wight had spoken, but hadn't caught his words, Hazel said: 'Pardon?'

As he hadn't meant for Hazel to hear him, Mr Wight hastily replied: 'Oh, nothing. It was nothing.'

The smile that Hazel had had since setting out to see Mr Wight disappeared. 'Oh, did I say something wrong? I was quite blunt in the way I talked about Mr Bellasis. I should know better. Ron was always telling me not to be so intense and direct. Sorry. Am I over-the-top?' she questioned.

'No! You're great! Whoever this Ron was, he couldn't have been more wrong. How could he say such a thing? What a daft person he must be. There's nothing better than a woman who just says it how it is,' Mr Wight assured Hazel.

The way Mr Wight spoke about Ron amused Hazel so much that a little giggle escaped her. 'He's my ex-husband,' she told him.

'Well, if that's what he said about you, no wonder he's your *ex*-husband. Why would you want to stay with someone like that?' Mr Wight said.

'Because being single is lonely, especially when you have no children as the man you were with at childbearing age didn't want them. He warned me I'd never find anyone else, and he was right. It's getting on for fifteen years now since we split,' Hazel replied.

The sadness in Hazel's voice found its way to Mr Wight's heart. It inspired him to reach out with his right hand and brush her cheek. Her gaze met his. When Mr Wight gently withdrew his hand, he smiled at her.

'There's a telly drama of that book you read. Would you like to come over one night to watch it with me? We could talk about how it compares to the book, and anything that pops into your head really,' Mr Wight offered.

'Really? I'd love that,' Hazel replied.

'Then I'll ask you over one evening,' Mr Wight said.

Having told Mr Wight how much she loved the book he'd recommended, which was what she'd set out to do, Hazel didn't know what to say. As standing in silence felt awkward to her, she told Mr Wight: 'I have to go now, George. Thanks for being so kind.'

'My pleasure, Hazel. It was lovely to see you!' Mr Wight called after Hazel as she scuttled off home.

Mr Wight stayed by his door to watch Hazel get to and go

through hers. When she was out of sight, he too went indoors. When he shut the door, his gaze settled on his hand, and he remembered how soft and smooth Hazel's cheek had felt when he'd stroked it.

It was only when Mr Wight strolled into his lounge that he remembered Mackenzie was there, and they'd been talking about Eddie and the antiques shop.

When he recalled what he'd spoken to Mackenzie about, something occurred to Mr Wight. 'If you only worked at the shop because your parents were worried about Eddie, do you want to keep doing it now you know they were wrong?' he asked.

'Well, that's something I wanted to talk to you about. I don't want to work for you anymore. It's nothing to do with you or Eddie though. I'm getting back together with Shaun, and we both want to be in Sheffield. Is that okay though? Don't you need me?' Mackenzie replied.

Mr Wight blushed. 'Actually, no. It works just fine with Eddie and I. I could do with someone else when he wants a holiday, but I can just hire a local youngster for that period. When you said you wanted to work for the family business, Eddie and me had to think up jobs for you to do so you felt helpful. That's why there's those three notebooks in the office. I need an inventory for insurance purposes, and just because it's sensible to know what you've got in stock, but I don't really need the others. What I buy for the business ends up on the inventory, unless it's for Eddie to mess with, and what we sell gets recorded by the till. It does only record the *amount* we sell each thing for, not what it was, but that's fine. There's no need to know the details of items we've sold. It was all just to give you something to do,' he revealed.

For the second time that day, Mackenzie felt stupid. She didn't dwell on that though, for what her grandad had told her meant that she could go up to Sheffield as soon as she wished guilt free.

Just to make sure she'd understood properly, Mackenzie

questioned: 'So you wouldn't mind if I went back Up North? Even if it was tomorrow? I have loved living with you, but I want to go home.'

'No, I don't mind. It's been nice having you around, but I can tell you don't belong down here. As nice as Colchester is, it isn't for you. I'm just happy for you that you're in love again,' Mr Wight said.

Delighted that she could have the future she wanted without upsetting her grandad, Mackenzie jumped up and hugged him.

49

Chapter Forty-nine

To take advantage of the good weather, Mackenzie asked Morton and Emma-Leigh to meet her and Shaun outside the castle. She made sure it coincided with Morton's lunch break.

When Mackenzie got to the castle, Morton and Emma-Leigh were already there, as was Shaun. It confused her that they were all together. Because she wanted to surprise them, she hadn't told her friends that she wanted to introduce them to Shaun. As she'd anticipated getting to the castle before him, she hadn't told Shaun what her friends looked like.

'The castle isn't even the oldest building in Colchester. There's a church that has a tower built when the Saxons still ruled, in ten fifty. There's even a Roman gateway from the second century tucked away down an alleyway,' Morton was telling Shaun.

Intrigued by the conversation her friend and boyfriend were having, Mackenzie kept just within earshot and hoped they wouldn't notice her. Emma-Leigh was messaging someone on her phone, so there was no chance of her spotting Mackenzie.

'Wow. All I can say about Sheffield, my home town, is that we invented stainless steel. Others sort of did it before us, but we were the first to do it properly,' Shaun said to Morton.

'Yes, around a hundred years ago, wasn't it?' Morton questioned.

'I wouldn't know. Facts aren't really my thing. Unless it concerns cricket. If you want to know what the score was at any test match England played in in the last ten years, I can probably tell you,' Shaun replied.

It amused Mackenzie that her boyfriend and friends were completely unaware of her and their surroundings. She decided she wouldn't interrupt, and would wait for one of them to notice her.

'I could do that for snooker finals at The Crucible,' Morton revealed.

'My girlfriend *loves* snooker. She's a decent player, too. Not many people get the best of her on the baize,' Shaun told Morton.

There was a pause before Morton answered. 'I know a woman from Sheffield who plays snooker. That woman asked myself and another of her friends to meet her here with less than twenty-four hours notice. Is your girlfriend Mackenzie by any chance? Has she asked us here to meet you?' he asked.

When Shaun's mouth fell open, Mackenzie took that as her cue to make her presence known. 'Well done, Morton. This is Shaun, my boyfriend. Shaun, you've been talking to Morton. Emma-Leigh is the girl on the phone with the immaculate eyebrows,' she revealed.

When Mackenzie opened her arms to him, Shaun rushed over and they embraced in front of her friends and random passers-by. Having been apart from her for a few hours, he wanted to snog her, but he settled for a peck on the cheek.

At some point when Shaun and Mackenzie were in each others arms, Emma-Leigh returned her phone to her bag and saw them. 'But I thought you loved Morton!' she cried.

Morton raised an eyebrow. 'Really? What made you think that? You don't even know she kissed me,' he asked.

'She kissed you?!' Emma-Leigh questioned.

The commotion between Morton and Emma-Leigh made Shaun and Mackenzie release each other. When she saw the look in Shaun's eyes, Mackenzie blushed. She hadn't expected him to find out about her alcohol-fuelled kiss.

'Yes, I did. I'd had far too much red wine, and confused the feeling of being drunk with love. What's worse is, when I stopped kissing Morton, I told him I didn't love him and just went indoors,' Mackenzie told Emma-Leigh.

Turning to Shaun, Mackenzie explained: 'Sorry. I'm not used to being that drunk. I promise that was all it was. I don't love Morton, and he doesn't love me. In fact, he said he hated my kiss.'

Having dealt with Emma-Leigh and Shaun, Mackenzie focused on Morton. 'I told Emma-Leigh I had feelings for you so she'd stop going on about getting me a new boyfriend. I was heartbroken, and in no mood to have a date with her auntie's cousin's son, or whoever it would have ended up being,' she explained to him.

Emma-Leigh emitted a short and shrill shriek. 'You lied? I was only trying to be nice!' she said.

Ignoring Emma-Leigh, Shaun chuckled. 'That's hilarious, that you confused being drunk with being in love. You never drink, so I can quite see how you did it. You must have been *bladdered*, because when you're sober, you're an *incredible* kisser,' he told Mackenzie.

'If you're back with Shaun, does that mean the whole cheating thing wasn't true? Did his parents lie?' Morton questioned.

'Yes! How did you know they'd lied? I didn't think someone's parents would make up such a thing about their own son,' Mackenzie asked.

Morton shrugged. 'All parents are different. I know for sure that some would say *anything* about their children. Not mine, thankfully, but some,' he replied.

A breeze blew through the park. The timing felt appropriate to Mackenzie. It gave her chills, as did thinking about Shaun's parents.

'So, if you and Shaun are an item now, does that mean you're leaving us to go back Up North?' Emma-Leigh asked.

It was the one bit of meeting up with her friends that Mackenzie had not been looking forward to. It was made slightly easier by Emma-Leigh asking. She'd worried that she'd have to randomly blurt out at some point that she may well never see Emma-Leigh again, and only see Morton a couple of times a year.

'Yes, I am. We plan to go up tomorrow,' Mackenzie revealed.

'Oh... Well, at least I get to meet him. That is why you asked us here, isn't it? To get to know Shaun?' Emma-Leigh questioned.

Pleased that Emma-Leigh seemed to be taking it well, Mackenzie smiled. 'That's exactly why. I've told you both about him, so I thought you should get to put a face to the name,' she explained.

With his hands in his pockets, Shaun's gaze wandered, taking in his surroundings. He wasn't exactly sure what his role was. Was he supposed to give Emma-Leigh and Morton a short version of his life story, or just discuss the weather with them?

Whilst looking around him, Shaun noticed that Morton also wasn't paying attention. He was twiddling his thumbs. When they'd eaten pizza in his hotel room after getting back from Bradwell Waterside, Mackenzie had told Shaun how much of a support Morton had been. It had sounded like they'd been close, though there was no hint of romance between them. Based purely on how he'd helped Mackenzie, Shaun liked Morton. He felt a little bit guilty about taking Mackenzie Up North away from him.

'I, erm... I need to... See you in a minute,' Morton stammered.

Before anyone could stop him, Morton hurried away into the park.

'Do you think he's okay?' Shaun asked Mackenzie.

'No, but I don't know what to do. I'll leave him for a minute and see if he comes back,' Mackenzie replied.

'He's probably just sad about you leaving. It's not like he has many friends, though of course you can see why. I'll message Cecilia later and have her warn Jude to keep an eye on Morton over the next few weeks,' Emma-Leigh said.

Mackenzie nodded. She knew Emma-Leigh was right. With the support of his Southerner friends, she hoped Morton would get over her departure quickly.

To move things on, Emma-Leigh clapped her hands together. 'I'm going to miss you too, but I'm not going to storm off. I'm just going to make the most of this last bit of time, and the chance to check Shaun is worthy of you,' Emma-Leigh told Mackenzie.

'Ooh, now I'm scared(!) Can I pass the Emma-Leigh test?' Shaun replied with a twinkle in his eye.

'We'll see. Let's start with your prospects. What is your job?' Emma-Leigh asked.

In full view of Emma-Leigh, Mackenzie and Shaun shared an amused smile.

As she knew her behaviour was amusing, Emma-Leigh thought nothing of the fact that Mackenzie and Shaun would probably laugh about her behind her back later.

'I work as a carpenter. I do have a degree in jewellery, materials, and design, which might impress you. It wasn't quite what I wanted, but I had to do *something* at uni. One day, I hope to be a master carpenter, which is a very well-paid job,' Shaun told Emma-Leigh.

'You didn't need to tell me about the degree. You had me at carpenter. That must mean you're good with your hands,' Emma-Leigh said with a smile.

'I can't say if I'm good with my hands. You'd have to ask Mackenzie if that's the case,' Shaun replied.

Mackenzie gasped. 'Shaun!' she cried incredulously.

Emma-Leigh chortled. 'Judging by the shade of red your cheeks have gone, I think he's *very* good with his hands,' she commented.

That comment prompted Mackenzie to dwell on what Shaun had done to her with his hands in the privacy of his hotel room just twelve hours ago. As she burned with a mix of desire and embarrassment, she tried to work out how to extract herself from the situation.

'Morton's been gone a while now. Why don't you check on him?' Shaun suggested.

Relief and a refreshing spring breeze cooled Mackenzie in an instant. 'Yes, I'll see if I can find him,' Mackenzie agreed.

When she realised Morton had headed in the direction of the public toilets, she made her way to them. She found him outside them. Water was trickling down from his puffy and red eyes.

'Oh, Morton! I'm sorry to have upset you this much!' Mackenzie cried.

Morton shook his head. 'I'm gutted that you're leaving, yet happy for you at the same time. There is a perplexing cocktail of thoughts and emotions in my head right now. These tears are nothing to do with *you* though. I won't let myself cry over you,' he replied.

That unsettled Mackenzie. What awful thing had happened to Morton?

Before Mackenzie could ask, Morton explained: 'These are happy tears. I got a phone call just over a minute ago to tell me I'm going to be a best man one day.'

Concern was replaced by elation, along with a heap of relief. 'Congratulations!' Mackenzie said.

'You know the couple. Not well enough to be invited, but you'll know their names. It's Jude and Cecilia,' Morton revealed.

'He popped the question? That's great for them, and for you.

They did seem so in love when I went round their house to borrow his car,' Mackenzie commented.

Morton laughed. 'You don't know the couple *that* well then. Yes, they are in love, but it wasn't him who proposed. Jude could never pluck up the courage to ask a woman as beautiful as Cecilia to marry him. *She* asked *him*. They were sitting on the sofa last night, just chatting, and she asked him to go and make her a cup of tea. When Jude came back into the lounge, Cecilia was down on one knee with a ring in her hand. He nearly spilled the tea apparently, but was just about able to put it down safely and say yes,' he told Mackenzie.

It was the simplest proposal Mackenzie had ever heard of. She hoped that, if Shaun ever proposed to her, he did it in a similar way. Rose petals, choirs singing ballads, and pretty views were unnecessary. The important part about the proposal was the question itself, which could be asked anywhere. If Shaun asked her to marry him on the balcony of a swanky hotel room with a string quartet playing love songs nearby, Mackenzie would probably refuse. As Shaun disliked fancy things, this was unlikely, but still she briefly imagined what it would be like if he did.

When Morton drew breath to speak, Mackenzie was brought back to the real world. 'Do you mind if I *don't* get to know Shaun? If I *like* him, then that's *two* marvellous people who I have to say goodbye to forever. If I *don't* like him and think he's atrocious, then I have to live with the knowledge that someone as wonderful as you is stuck with an ignoramus. It just doesn't make sense to me,' he said.

Mackenzie nodded. 'I understand. I really am sorry to leave you,' she agreed.

'I am thrilled for you that you've got Shaun back. You deserve to be in a relationship with someone you love as deeply as him, and you don't need to apologise for it. I just wish it didn't mean I'll never see you again. I am aware that's selfish, but I *feel* quite selfish at the moment. As I'm losing the closest friend I've had, besides Jude perhaps, I can forgive myself for being morose and self-centred,' Morton told Mackenzie.

Some of the pain Morton was feeling was shared by Mackenzie. She also wished going home with the man she loved didn't mean leaving Morton behind. She'd had an idea that made it a bit better, and she shared it with Morton. 'I forgive you being selfish too. Anyone would feel the way you do. They just wouldn't necessarily admit it. You *will* see me again though. One of the things we bonded over is snooker. My home is the home of snooker. As long as Jude and Cecilia don't choose then to get married, why not come up for the World Championship? I've watched at least a few matches at The Crucible every year since I was ten, but the only person I've had to go with is my dad, and now even he doesn't go. Shaun only likes cricket, so I can't take him. I'd love to share The Crucible with you. There's nothing like the atmosphere at the final session of the final match,' Mackenzie said.

'Really? I've never been to The Crucible. I've always wanted to, but I didn't fancy going all that way alone. You could always come down for The Masters. I know Alexandra Palace is hardly on the doorstep, but we're closer to London here than you are in Sheffield,' Morton replied.

It had already occurred to Mackenzie that she could return to The South for The Masters and to see Morton in Colchester. 'That's a plan then. We can get together for The Masters and the World Championship. Now all we need is a friend in York so we can go to the UK Championship with a local too,' Mackenzie declared.

Morton smiled. 'On that happy note, shall we say goodbye? There's not going to be a better moment than this,' he suggested.

'I guess so. Thank you, Morton, for being such a good friend. Look after yourself until we meet again,' Mackenzie said.

'It was a pleasure. Thank you, too. Farewell, Mackenzie,' Morton replied.

With Mackenzie watching him go, Morton strolled off into the park.

When Morton was out of sight, Mackenzie turned away from the public toilets and headed back to the castle.

As Mackenzie approached him and Emma-Leigh, Shaun was saying: 'Her simplicity is her best feature. Some people are so complicated and conniving. They play games for attention and lie for the fun of it. Not Mackenzie. If *she* wants attention, she'll tell you. If she's lying, she has a good reason to do so.'

'Hi, I want attention. I'm not lying,' Mackenzie said.

Shaun blushed. 'You heard that?' he asked.

When Mackenzie nodded and grinned at him, Shaun's cheeks turned even redder.

'Where is Morton? Did you not find him? We can't just let him wander off all alone when he's upset. Do we need to start a search party?' Emma-Leigh asked.

'It's alright. I found him by the loos. We had a chat, and he won't be rejoining us, but he *is* okay,' Mackenzie assured Emma-Leigh.

'Oh, that's good,' Emma-Leigh replied.

It reassured Mackenzie that Emma-Leigh was concerned about Morton. She was sure it wouldn't just be Jude keeping an eye on him.

Emma-Leigh gasped. 'Ooh, I've just thought of something. As Morton isn't with us, can we shop? Shaun told me you love vintage clothes, and I know a great shop in the Lanes for vintage. It's not my style, but I've heard good things about the place. Shopping together would be the perfect end to our friendship. Please can we shop?' she asked.

To check Shaun wouldn't mind being dragged around a vintage clothes shop, Mackenzie glanced across at him. When he nodded, she said: 'That sounds perfect. Lead the way.'

50

Chapter Fifty

As Mackenzie had hoped she would, Emma-Leigh took her to Bygones, a place she had once walked past and admired.

When she entered the shop and saw the rails of dresses and jackets that had been loved by people who'd lived through a completely different time, Mackenzie let out a contented sigh.

'This is your happy place, isn't it?' Emma-Leigh asked.

'There's so much,' Mackenzie whispered.

The bright red colour of a jacket from the 1940s drew Mackenzie towards it. She gently separated it from all the clothes around it and removed it from the rail so she could truly appreciate its beauty.

To assist Mackenzie with shopping, Emma-Leigh dashed over.

When he was sure Emma-Leigh and the rails of clothes would keep Mackenzie occupied, Shaun disappeared into the aisles of cabinets full of little treasures.

'I wonder how someone who wore this would have lived,' Mackenzie mused aloud.

'Is that why you love vintage? Because of the history?' Emma-Leigh asked.

Holding the red jacket against herself, Mackenzie replied: 'Partly. I do love how it looks on me though.'

When Emma-Leigh recalled her meetings with Mackenzie, she couldn't think of a time she'd seen her in a vintage outfit. She usually wore a modern t-shirt and trousers, or a long skirt. It suddenly occurred to her that Mackenzie may not be able to afford the clothes she loved. In that case, being in Bygones would be torture for her.

'Sorry, I never thought to check if you can afford this. You never wear vintage, so I suppose you can't,' Emma-Leigh said.

Mackenzie smiled. 'Don't worry. I can more than afford this. The only reason I've clad myself in mass-produced modern stuff is I haven't felt like myself, so I didn't want to dress like myself,' she explained.

Delighted that money wasn't an issue, Emma-Leigh cried: 'Then let us stop talking and start searching for beauties!'

—

As she and Mackenzie rummaged through the rails, Emma-Leigh began to get an idea of what Mackenzie liked. This meant that, when she spotted a navy-blue suit, she had a feeling she'd like it.

'What about this?' Emma-Leigh asked, holding the navy suit up for Mackenzie to see.

The speed at which Mackenzie came dashing over confirmed Emma-Leigh's suspicions.

When she reached Emma-Leigh, Mackenzie carefully took the suit from her hands and checked the label inside. 'I knew it! It's Lilli Ann,' she said.

'Is that special?' Emma-Leigh asked.

'Very. They're famous for quality suits and coats with classic silhouettes. I like them because they helped to keep some French factories in business after the Second World War,' Mackenzie revealed.

In the twenty minutes or so they'd spent looking through vintage clothes, Emma-Leigh felt like she'd bonded with Mackenzie more than she had in the rest of their friendship. Understanding her style helped Emma-Leigh understand who Mackenzie was as a person. She now knew Mackenzie was understated and classy, but liked to be noticed.

When her phone dinged to inform her that she'd received a message, Emma-Leigh murmured to Mackenzie: 'I'll just be a minute.'

'I see. You can keep an eye on the things we've picked out while I look for a fitting room,' Mackenzie replied.

Totally absorbed by her phone, Emma-Leigh didn't see Mackenzie wander off. All she was aware of was a message from Cecilia, asking if she was free that evening to come over for a glass of prosecco and a chat. As Ronnie was away on business, and she wanted to talk to Jude about Morton, Emma-Leigh agreed. It was rare that Cecilia invited her over. She wondered if she had news of some kind. When she read the message again, she saw Cecilia had mentioned Tamsyn was also invited. That made Emma-Leigh think they were gathering to celebrate something Tamsyn had achieved at work.

After getting distracted by Facebook, Emma-Leigh put her phone away and spotted Mackenzie waving at her from one corner of the shop. She gathered up all the clothes and carried them over to Mackenzie, where she was waiting by the fitting room with Shaun and a woman who introduced herself as Helen, the owner of the shop.

When Mackenzie came out in her first outfit, the navy-blue Lilli Ann suit, Shaun was reminded of how much vintage suited her. When they'd been together, she'd only had a few pieces. What she had, she'd had to find cheap on online auction sites. He was delighted on her behalf that she could now have whatever she wanted.

He was delighted on his own behalf that she looked ravishing in the clothes she loved.

Dressing up in vintage clothes and showing them to Shaun made Mackenzie feel more like herself than she ever had. When she decided to take everything and left Bygones with paper bags full of wearable treasures that Helen had carefully packed, Mackenzie felt like she was carrying pieces of her soul. Having a new wardrobe for her new life seemed appropriate.

Whenever she finished shopping, Emma-Leigh was sad. She was even more sad that day though, because it meant it was time to say goodbye to Mackenzie. 'I guess this is it,' she said.

Mackenzie shook her head. 'Not quite. I have something for you. I got it when you were on your phone,' she replied.

As the something was concealed in her jacket pocket, and her hands were holding bags, Mackenzie couldn't get to it.

Seeing Mackenzie's predicament, Shaun took the bags from her with a smile.

When Mackenzie reached into her pocket and pulled out a brooch that depicted a basket of flowers in silver on a royal blue enamel background, Emma-Leigh gasped. As Mackenzie placed it in her hands, she could barely breathe. She hadn't expected her to get her anything, let alone something so elegant and eye-catching.

'The blue enamel is bright and captures your attention. Then you have the sparkle from the marcasite around the edge, and the detail of the basket in silver. It made me think of you, so I thought it would be the perfect goodbye present,' Mackenzie explained.

'I think I'm in love. Thank you,' Emma-Leigh told Mackenzie, gazing at the brooch she'd given her.

As he reached a hand into his pocket, Shaun announced: 'It's not just Emma-Leigh who gets a present. While you were distracted by clothes, I picked up something for you.'

'But you didn't have to. I'm the one with the money. I can get whatever I want,' Mackenzie pointed out.

When Shaun produced a necklace with a Roman coin pendant, Mackenzie fell silent. 'No, I didn't have to, but I wanted to. The pendant is cast from an ancient coin. It isn't an authentic one. That's how I could afford it. I'm really pleased that we're going back to Sheffield, but I know Colchester has been important to you, and I wanted to get something to commemorate your time here,' he explained.

The replica coin swung back and forth in the breeze, which to Mackenzie represented the variety of emotions she'd experienced in Colchester. To take her gift from Shaun, Mackenzie reached out. When their hands touched, Mackenzie said to him: 'So much has happened down here. As important as it's been though, Colchester is not Sheffield. It never could have been, and never will be. Home is where the heart is.'

Acknowledgements

Thank you, reader, for giving me the opportunity to share with you the characters in my head and the things they get up to. To me, characters in books are friends (not just in my own books), and it is a pleasure to introduce you to the people who occupy my thoughts for many hours a day.

At its best, when people are kind and it is used correctly, social media is a wonderful thing. I'd like to take this opportunity to thank the kind people who follow me on Instagram and Facebook. When it comes to connecting with my fellow authors and readers, Facebook groups are particularly useful. They allow me to promote my own novels and share my love for other peoples' brilliant books. Stay Bookish and Bitchy Bookworms are two groups that I am quite active in.

There's one group on Facebook that is particularly special. It is so special that it deserves its own paragraph. Heidi Swain and Friends – A Facebook Book Club, is a warm and welcoming community dedicated to all things Heidi Swain and her fun-filled books. Thanks to Heidi, and the admins Sue and Fiona, it is more than that. It's a space to discuss other authors' books, and mental health, and cats, and many other things. I know I'm not the only one who appreciates this lovely group of people.

In addition to her hard work as admin of several Facebook groups, Sue Baker writes beautiful reviews. She very kindly allowed me to use part of her review of Home Is Where the Heart Is on the new cover.

To celebrate love and romance authors on Valentine's Day, Fiona organised a giveaway in Heidi Swain and Friends. One of the prizes was the opportunity to name a character in this book. Thank you to Miriam O'Brien, who gave me the names Pixie Lynch and Misty O'Brien.

One of the things that is occasionally discussed in Heidi Swain and Friends is television (yes, that is a bit of a tenuous link). Some aspects of Home Is Where the Heart is were inspired by things I've watched. Eddie's upcycling business is inspired by Money for Nothing, Mackenzie's love of vintage clothes was inspired by an episode of Bargain Hunt, her career as an architect was partly inspired by Grand Designs, and Hazel's passion for gardening was partly inspired by Garden Rescue. Thank you to everyone involved in those programs for entertaining me, educating me, and for helping me work out who my characters are and what they do.

Sometimes something I watch prompts me to do some research on the internet. For example, when Bargain Hunt mentioned the fashion label Lilli Ann, I felt the need to know more about it. The information I find on the web tells me what you can do in the garden in May, that you can study architecture at The University of Sheffield, and so much more. Thank you to Google, The Metro, UCAS, The University of Sheffield, Simon Gill Architects, RHS, Homes and Gardens, Redburlwood.com, Autotrader, Colchester Zoo, Colchester Borough Council, Leeds City Council, Palette London, and

Acknowledgements - 247

Chronically Vintage for their webpages full of inspiration and information.

Most of the businesses in my books are fictional, but inspired by real ones. It makes things easier. In this book, there's an exception to this. Tea Rose Cafe really exists, as does Shirley the waitress. I had such a good time there last summer that I decided the cafe, its courtyard, and its lovely and efficient waitress, had to be in one of my books. Thank you to Tea Rose Cafe and its staff for great food and even better service.

Thank you to Shaun Murphy, for being one of the nicest and most entertaining players in the 2021 Snooker World Championship, which I watched while working on this book. Also thank you to Shaun Murphy for having a nice name that I used in this book.

Thank you to Jason Manford, for supporting the little guy, whether that's a lesser-known support act, a small theatre, or a self-published author. Most of all, thank you for the best night I've had this year so far.

My mum deserves thanks and praise for many things, most of which have nothing to do with books. In these acknowledgements, I'd like to thank her for being supportive of my writing, and taking me to see Jason Manford. It means the world to me, and I am so lucky to have been born to you.

Finally, thanks again to my readers for reading all of this as well as a 60,000+ word novel.

Other Books By Michaela Trueman

Cue Romance

Their eyes meet across a snooker table... or so Jude thought. In reality, Cecilia, the stunning blonde who's caught his eye is looking at the ball she wants to pot. She hasn't even noticed Jude, but he's noticed her. Cue Romance is a tale of fun, friendship, and love under a mostly-sunny and sometimes seagull-filled Essex sky.

The Christmas Genie's Wish

When a friendly and dedicated person, with a creative mind and a good knowledge of the local businesses and their stock and services is required to fulfill the role of Christmas Genie (a personal shopper with a less dull title), there's just one girl for the job.

All year round, Eugenie Holland dresses up the people of Colchester in the contemporary clothes that her aunt's boutique stocks. Putting a smile on customer's faces puts a smile on hers. This makes her the perfect person to be The Christmas Genie.

While helping other people buy presents, The Christmas Genie herself finds the very thing she wants for Christmas. He ticks every box of her wishlist, but will he be present on Christmas Day?

Fool Me Thrice

Whilst queueing in the supermarket to buy ingredients to cook a special dinner for her gorgeous long-term boyfriend, Ronnie, Emma-Leigh sees an advert for a blind dating event inspired by her favourite TV show. As she is already very much in love, she scrolls past it. A few hours later, she finds her beloved in bed with another woman. The friend she stays the night with convinces the unexpectedly newly-single Emma-Leigh to sign up for the dating event whilst watching the show it was inspired by with her.

The very thought of Ronnie, makes Emma-Leigh sick, let alone the idea of sharing a house with him, so she returns to the village where she grew up. There she finds squabbling sisters, a disapproving mother, and a long list of household tasks to complete in lieu of rent. Geographically, Writtle is more than twenty miles from Ronnie and her life with him, but moving on mentally is as hard as commuting along the busy A12 every day for work.

The experience she's had leaves Emma-Leigh believing she cannot trust any man and will never fall in love again. Can anyone challenge this view and prove her wrong, or will her spirits remain as damp as the autumn leaves that cover the paths of Hylands Park.

Millie's Snuggly & Toasty Christmas

One cold December day, Jude finds his sister, Millie, shivering on his doorstep, suitcases in hand. Jude is willing to listen and help Millie, but she isn't ready to share what caused her to flee from Cambridge. All that's clear is Millie needs Jude.

Floyd is reluctant to replace the troublesome housemate who has finally moved out. He's more interested in finding The One. Unfortunately for him, his bank balance is very keen on splitting the rent with someone, and dating doesn't bring in money.

Can Jude and his loved ones sieve out the truth? Will Millie manage to open up to someone? Is a problem shared truly a problem halved or will Millie's life become even more complicated this winter?
Find out in this heart-warming, sweet, and Christmassy tale.

Social Media

I like to interact with my fellow readers and writers. If you like giveaways, have any pictures with my books, want to stay up to date with my writing and I, or have any comments to make, please get in touch. I can be found on Facebook and Instagram.

LIKE AND FOLLOW MY FACEBOOK PAGE, MICHAELA TRUEMAN - AUTHOR.

FOLLOW ME ON INSTAGRAM @MICHAELA_TRUEMAN_AUTHOR

I'm also on Goodreads and Amazon's Author Central. If you enjoyed reading this book, or even if you didn't, please, please, please leave a review on Amazon or Goodreads. Positive or negative, long or short, reviews help me, and your fellow readers.

Excerpt

Here's the first couple of chapters of my debut novel, Cue Romance. You may notice some familiar faces.

Chapter One

If Jude aimed his shot correctly, he was sure to defeat Morton. If it missed, Jude's hopes of getting one up on his long-time foe would be dashed.

To ensure it was successful, Jude focused his mind and looked down the line of his shot. It looked perfect, so he drew a deep breath and took the shot. The white ball rolled across the table and smashed into the black ball, which rattled in the jaws.

'Ha! You lose yet again!' Morton crowed.

Jude didn't hear his friend jeer at him. He was still down on his shot, looking at the intriguing blonde who was the reason he'd missed it.

The game of snooker, which Jude and Morton were playing, requires its players to bend over vast cloth-covered tables and stare intently at the ball they intend to hit with the cue ball, which they hit with their cue, a long wooden stick. That was how Jude had ended up in an impromptu staring contest with the woman playing on the next table. He stood stock-still, gazing into the woman's blue eyes, while she gazed right back at him, standing in a similar position to him.

Because only two of the six tables were in use, and they were being used by three quiet people, the snooker room at the Colneside was silent. The temporary silence in the room was broken by the soft donk of a cue striking the cue ball, followed by the click of the cue ball making contact with the object ball, and the growl of frustration from the woman who had set that chain of events in motion. She immediately stood up, thus breaking eye contact with Jude, who realised the woman had been staring at the ball she'd been aiming to pot, not him. There had never been a staring contest, but if there had been one, he'd have won it.

'Go on then. Humiliate me yet again,' Jude said to Morton, walking away from the table to let him take his shot.

A great deal of noise came from the table next to the one Morton was playing on because the woman using it was setting all the balls up again, but that didn't put him off his shot. He sent the black ball spinning nine feet across the baize and into the corner pocket with perfect accuracy.

'Did you mean like that?' Morton asked.

'Yup. Pretty much that,' Jude confirmed.

Morton glanced at his watch. 'We've got plenty of time left. Shall we set up again?' he suggested.

'That's cool with me. I'll do the baulk colours. As you're the one who potted most of them, you can do the reds and the colours down your end,' Jude agreed.

The pair strolled to their respective ends of the table to do just that. As he walked, it occurred to Morton that something was wrong with what Jude had said, and he couldn't help but mention it. 'Actually, you potted more of the balls. You took lower value colours with your reds, so although your score was lower than mine, you scored it with more balls,' he pointed out.

In response, Jude stuck his tongue out and said: 'Dweeb.'

Instead of continuing to insult Morton, Jude put all his concentration into putting the yellow, brown, and green balls on the white spots marked for them on the snooker table.

At the opposite end of the table, Morton was methodically

putting the fifteen red balls into the wooden triangle provided for them.

On the table next to Jude and Morton, the woman playing on it had finished setting it up. She placed the cue ball precisely where she wanted it, next to the brown ball, and bent double over the snooker table. Full of hope, but not much confidence, the woman struck the cue ball with the battered cue she'd picked up from the rack on the wall by her table. She stayed bent over the table to watch the cue ball merrily roll straight past the triangle of reds it was supposed to glance off, bounce off of a couple of the cushions at the edge of the table, and come straight back to her. 'Seriously!' she yelled.

The sheer frustration in the one word the woman spoke, and the volume she spoke it in, attracted the attention of Jude and Morton. They glanced in her direction and saw she had her head in her hands. 'I can't do this. I just can't do this,' they heard her mutter to herself.

'Erm, don't wanna intrude or nothing, but are you alright?' Jude couldn't help asking the woman.

'Oh, I'm sorry for bothering you. I'm fine, just most frustrated that I can't do this,' the woman replied.

Jude and Morton looked at each other. Morton raised an eyebrow as if he was asking a question, but Jude didn't know what the question was. When Jude didn't answer the question, whatever it was, Morton tutted and turned his attention to the woman. 'Would you like me to give you a few pointers? I've been doing this a long time and I've learnt a lot over that time. I can't impart my wealth of knowledge to Jude here, because he just won't listen, but you'd probably be a more willing pupil,' Morton offered.

Only then did Jude realise that Morton's unspoken question to him had been: "Shall we help her?".

While the woman was considering Morton's offer, a man and woman entered the snooker room, kissing each other noisily as they walked. They made their way to the end table, which thankfully was as far away from Jude and Morton as possible.

'That would be most helpful. Thank you,' the woman who Morton had spoken to replied.

A smile appeared on Morton's face. 'Fantabulous! I'm Morton, by the way, and my friend here is called Jude,' Morton said.

'My name is Cecilia,' said the woman, who was called Cecilia.

As it happened, Morton had more than "a few" pointers. He critiqued and tweaked every part of Cecilia's game, from her stance, to where she placed her left hand on the table. He also talked her through what to consider when deciding what shot to play.

Much to Morton's delight, Cecilia listened to his every word and did exactly as she was told. After an hour's intensive tuition, Cecilia felt much more confident and capable in the game of snooker.

While Morton coached Cecilia, Jude stood nonchalantly in the background and watched him do it. It was his intention to say something clever and funny to impress the alluring Cecilia, but he didn't get the chance as she was completely and utterly focused on what Morton was teaching her. That was probably for the best because despite having an hour to think about it, Jude didn't come up with anything clever or funny to say.

Jude, Morton, and Cecilia only became aware of the time when the woman of the once-noisily kissing couple mentioned how late it was and suggested that, as they both had uni tomorrow, they really should go to bed. The man of the couple replied: 'You mean together, right?' That inspired the woman to kiss him noisily again.

'I definitely should head home. I've got piles of work to get through tomorrow,' Cecilia said.

Jude nodded thoughtfully. 'Yeah, and I've got to see a client in the morning,' he added.

As if agreeing, Morton yawned. 'Then we should all pay up and return to our respective homes,' he declared.

'Thank you, guys. I'm most grateful for the tips you gave me, Morton, and you, poor Jude, must have been bored standing around by yourself because I'd taken your friend away from you,' Cecilia said

'I usually am bored when I'm out with Morton,' Jude commented.

Cecilia chuckled to herself. 'Goodnight, guys,' she said, walking out of the snooker room.

A minute later, after downing their vodka and colas, Jude and Morton followed in Cecilia's footsteps.

'Same again next week, my friend?' Morton asked Jude while they stood at the snooker club bar, waiting to pay.

'Yup, just like every week,' Jude agreed.

Chapter Two

'Hey, Cecilia!' Jude called to Cecilia when she walked into the snooker room at the Colneside half an hour after he and Morton had.

Behind Cecilia, a young woman with short ginger hair and long legs who looked a couple of years younger than her companion walked in. 'Ah, do you know these men?' the ginger girl asked in a thick West Country accent.

'Vaguely. Morton, on the left, helped me improve my game, and Jude, with the brown curly hair and grey eyes, waited patiently while he did so,' Cecilia told her companion.

The ginger girl nodded. 'Nice to meet you, Jude and Morton. I'm Tamsyn,' she said.

'One day to be Tamsyn Menadue BA (Hons),' Cecilia added.

Tamsyn blushed. 'Well, I don't know about that,' she replied.

With the intention of making Cecilia laugh, Jude bowed low. 'A pleasure to make your acquaintance, Miss Menadue, one day to be BA (Hons),' he said.

A quiet titter came from Cecilia, but Tamsyn just silently folded her arms. 'I assume that was meant to be funny,' she said.

'Yup, it was. Didn't quite work out how I hoped,' Jude replied.

'Well I was amused,' Cecilia told Jude.

'Good. It was my aim to amuse you. Beautiful women like you deserve to be amused,' Jude revealed.

'Beautiful?' Cecilia questioned.

A slight smile broke out on Jude's face. 'Yeah. You're beautiful, among other things I imagine. I'm single, among other things,' he replied.

While wondering how to answer that, Cecilia felt Tamsyn tugging at her arm. She let herself be dragged to the snooker table next to Jude and Morton's, which was already lit for their use.

'Right then. Shall we get back to business? It was your shot, I believe,' Morton said to Jude, forcing him to turn his attention back to the game.

Giving Cecilia one last wistful look, Jude walked around his snooker table and got down on his shot.

Like last week, Jude was distracted by the table next to him, so couldn't concentrate on his own game. He noticed that Cecilia was playing a little better than the week before, and she was a lot calmer.

At one point, after Tamsyn missed a shot for the third time, she burst out laughing, and Cecilia tittered with her.

'Thank you for coming with me to practice,' Cecilia said to Tamsyn when their laughter had subsided.

'We both know you asked me here for my benefit, for which I'm extremely grateful. The last thing I felt like doing after that phone call was studying, but that's exactly what I'd have done if you hadn't called,' Tamsyn replied.

'Then it suits both of us,' Cecilia declared.

After five attempts, Tamsyn played her shot correctly and so it was Cecilia's turn to play. All Tamsyn had been able to do was hit a red ball; she hadn't been able to put the cue ball somewhere where Cecilia wouldn't be able to pot. She had left a straight pot to the middle pocket. In the game of snooker, pots didn't get much easier than that, so Cecilia was furious with herself when she hit the red just off centre, sending it to one side of the pocket.

'I'm awful! Conner is sure to laugh at me!' Cecilia cried.

'You're not awful. Even if you were, it's just a game,' Tamsyn told Cecilia.

'A game Conner is sure to beat me at,' Cecilia replied.

Tamsyn shrugged. 'If he beats you, and if he laughs at you, just remember that it says so much more about him then it does about you,' she said.

A wave of guilt suddenly overcame Cecilia. 'I'm sorry for moaning about family. They're nothing compared to yours,' she replied.

'True, but mine are three hundred miles away. Of course, that doesn't stop my mother calling me up out of the blue to ask: "When are you going to find yourself a nice guy, or even a girl. We'd understand you know, if it's a girl. We get that is part of the modern world that we live in now. Perhaps that's why you still haven't found someone. You're one of those lesbian people",' Tamsyn pointed out, hamming up her accent when she quoted her mother.

Even that short snippet of Tamsyn's phone call with her mother angered Cecilia. 'They're lucky that they live three hundred miles away, for it makes it too difficult for me to drive to their house and strangle them,' she growled.

Tamsyn cackled at the idea of Cecilia strangling her parents. 'Well, that would give me resus practice I suppose,' she said.

Even though Jude knew eavesdropping was rude, he couldn't help listening to every word of Cecilia and Tamsyn's conversation. He was in fact so tuned in to them that he didn't hear Morton asking him a question. He did hear him when he hissed in his ear: 'Did you not notice that she completely ignored it when you said you were single? Sorry, but she's not interested, my friend.'

'Like you know anything about relationships. Remind me, how long have you been single? Twenty-one years, ain't it?' Jude retorted.

Colour drained from Morton's face. 'Um, well... that is true, but it's... well it's just...,' he stammered.

'An incredibly mean thing to say?' Jude suggested.

Morton nodded, but still couldn't find the words.

Some people might hug at this moment, but Jude wasn't much of a hugger. Instead of hugging the now-miserable Morton, he half-heartedly slapped him on the back. 'I don't mean to upset you. I were just joshing with you, you know? I don't think sometimes before I open my gob,' Jude told his friend.

A slight smile appeared on Morton's face. 'That... that is very... really true,' he agreed.

'What's best for you now? Do you want to carry on or is it better to call the whole thing off?' Jude asked.

'Go home. This isn't going to... to go away,' Morton replied.

That was the answer Jude had expected. He knew Morton well, and he knew when his stammer made an appearance, it ruined everything for him, even his beloved snooker. That was why Jude felt sick with guilt for inadvertently causing Morton to stammer.

'Okay then. I'll collect the balls, take them back to the man and pay up, so you can go if you like. I'll see you next week, if you wanna see me next week, that is,' Jude said.

'Yes, just like every week,' Morton replied.

www.ingramcontent.com/pod-product-compliance
Lightning Source LLC
Chambersburg PA
CBHW071226080526
44587CB00013BA/1509